ADVANCE PRAISE

This book will light a fire in your heart and soul. You will suddenly realize the importance of making more money than you need, because it isn't about the money—it is about what the money can do.

—MO ANDERSON, AUTHOR OF *A JOY-FILLED LIFE*

Myra is a Money Ninja! She has mastered the art of money (how to make it, how to keep it, and how to build wealth). The passion, principles, mindset, and skills you will learn in this book were born deep in Myra's DNA. She was born to write this book. Myra and her husband, Rick, have accumulated over thirty rental properties, a retirement stock portfolio, multiple businesses, and most importantly, are 100 percent debt-free! If you apply the principles in this book, you can build that wealthy, debt-free lifestyle!

—JIM AND LINDA MCKISSACK, KELLER WILLIAMS
OHIO VALLEY REGION OWNERS, AUTHORS OF *HOLD:
HOW TO FIND, BUY, AND RENT HOUSES FOR WEALTH*

Wow! In this new book, Myra brings you the cold, hard truth. The path to financial independence is a narrow road, and you will have to deny yourself some of the temporary pleasures of this world until you build some momentum first. But here is the good news! She shares with you not only her stories but also her secrets to encourage you to become financially free! Myra has inspired me for years to be more conscious of my own personal spending and see the big financial picture with my own real estate investments. She brings her southern, no-nonsense style to a subject normally reserved for investment "elites" and breaks things down in a super-practical, easy-to-understand format. I am excited for a new generation of possibility thinkers to get ahold of this book and implement these strategies. Thank you, Myra, for investing in all of us, too!

—Derek Tye, Real Estate Investor, Real Estate Sales Business Owner, Past President of The Southern Ohio Association of Realtors, Author

Money helps create freedom and gives you choice. In this book, Myra will show you how to use money to create a life worth living for you and your family.

—David Osborn, *New York Times* Best-Selling Author of *Wealth Can't Wait*

DOWN HOME MONEY

Down Home Money

A *Simple* Approach *to* FINANCIAL FREEDOM

Myra Oliver

LIONCREST
PUBLISHING

DOWN HOME MONEY

A Simple Approach to Financial Freedom

ISBN   978-1-5445-1473-4 *Hardcover*

       978-1-5445-1472-7 *Paperback*

       978-1-5445-1471-0 *Ebook*

To my best friend, confidant, and soulmate, Rick Oliver.
Thank you for being on this journey with me. I can't
imagine doing this thing called life without you.

In memory of Milton R. Williams, my beloved father. I followed your footsteps and became an author. I'm so grateful to be your daughter.

Contents

Disclaimer

This book and its contents are for your personal use only and are protected by applicable copyright, patent, and trademark laws. This book is presented solely for educational and entertainment purposes. The author and publisher are not offering it as legal, financial, accounting, or other professional services advice. The author and publisher make no representation or warranty, expressed or implied, as to the accuracy, completeness, or correctness of this book's opinions, analyses, or information, and assume no liabilities of any kind with respect to the accuracy or completeness of the contents. Neither the author nor the publisher shall be held liable or responsible to any person or entity with respect to any loss or incidental or consequential damages caused, or alleged to have been caused, directly or indirectly, by the information contained herein or in connection with an investor's reliance on or use of this book. No warranty may be created or extended by sales representatives or written sales materials.

Every person's situation is different, and the advice and strategies contained herein may not be suitable for your situation. You are responsible for your own investment decisions, and each investor is solely responsible for analyzing and evaluating any information used or relied upon in making an investment decision. Before making any investment decision, you should thoroughly investigate the proposed investment, consider your personal situation, and consult with a qualified advisor. The information and opinions provided in this book should not be relied upon or used as a substitute for consultation with professional advisors. As with all investments, past performance is not a guarantee of future results. The use of or reliance on the contents of this book is done solely at your own risk.

Foreword

I would like to introduce you to the youngest of my three children, Myra Oliver. As a child, Myra was tomboyish, a tall plain-Jane type with long, blonde, straight stringy hair. She had simple tastes with no froufrou, unlike her sister who loved frills and bows.

As Myra grew older, it became quite apparent that she looked nothing like her siblings—so apparent that someone suggested that she might have been adopted. We assured Myra that she was ours, but she needed proof. We could not find her birth certificate and had to call Frankfort, Kentucky, to request a copy. To this day, one of Myra's favorite sayings is "Documentation beats conversation," and it started here.

As the years rolled by, Myra became more independent and savvy. Sometimes money was extremely tight, and we would borrow lunch money from frugal Myra, who always managed to save for a rainy day. I might add that we borrowed at a very high interest rate!

Helping others and caring about their welfare is Myra's strong suit. Many nights, I would hear her counseling friends over the phone. We had to get her a private line and set a time limit to remind her she had school the next morning.

Myra did well in school and participated in several clubs and cheerleading. Her dad fondly called her Miss Everything in reference to her many achievements: Miss TCHS, Homecoming Queen, FFA Sweetheart, and the list goes on. She was well liked by her peers and teachers. She always had a smile and a positive attitude and included everyone regardless of status. Myra always wanted to make a difference, and she made it happen.

College wasn't for Myra. She chose a different path by becoming a hairstylist, which was a logical choice since her grandmother cut hair for many years. Myra was an excellent hairstylist, and she owned her own salon until she sold the business and retired at the ripe old age of thirty-three. Here I was still working, but my daughter retired before me because of how smart she had been with her money. Myra had been planning her retirement since she was twelve years old, and she made it happen.

After a three-year sabbatical, Myra started a new career in real estate. This path allowed Myra to find her real joy and passion for helping others. It also helped mold and prepare her for who God made her to be: a true inspirational leader.

Myra is from an entrepreneurial family. We were always open to new ideas to make money. These business ventures exposed us to inspirational, positive, successful people like Zig Ziglar, Jim Rohn, and Rich DeVos, who certainly rubbed off on Myra.

At age twenty-two, Myra lost her father, Milton R. Williams, to cancer. He was a huge influence in her life. Milton was a teacher, an avid Indian relic and coin collector, and a motivational speaker with a vibrant personality. He, too, was a published author and would be so proud to see Myra following his footsteps.

Now Myra is ready to put all that life has taught her into words to help you create your own financial freedom journey. Through this book, Myra is giving you a well-traveled, well-documented map to lead you in the right direction.

Best of luck in your financial freedom endeavor. Life is short, so live it to the fullest! I have had a front-row seat watching all of Myra's work, and I know if you really want change and are willing to put in the work, you too will have freedom to live your best life.

Happy freedom trails and with love,

Myra's mom, Peggy

Introduction

Imagine being able to live life on your terms. Imagine being able to spend as much time as you want with the people you love, doing the things that give you joy and satisfaction. Imagine living completely debt-free. Sound like something you'd enjoy? You can! But first, you have to address the thing that might be holding you back.

Financial problems are one of the most common struggles in America today. According to one survey, over 75 percent of the population lives paycheck to paycheck, and 71 percent of all workers say they are currently in debt.[1]

One of the primary reasons people struggle financially is that incomes do not run parallel with lifestyles. We spend more than we make. We use lines of credit to buy things we can't afford. We use credit cards to get things right now, even if we don't actually have the money in the bank to pay for them.

We live in a generation of consumerism and debt because we don't know the meaning of delayed gratification. When people buy things they cannot afford, they are really spending their future income—money they haven't even made yet. Then they have to stay at jobs they don't enjoy to pay for all the stuff they bought on credit. This is the debt trap so many Americans find themselves in.

Does this sound familiar? Are bills piling up with no end in sight? Are you drowning in debt and feeling stuck in a downward spiral? I have great news: you can make choices right now to change your current and future financial situation. Money is a tool that gives you options, but you have to make good choices. I'm going to show you how!

Before you can make changes, however, you have to want change. In other words, the pain of staying the same has to be greater than the pain of changing. The plan I offer in this book requires work. It's simple, but it's not easy. You have to be willing to address the real issue, which is you! It's easier to blame other things or people, but that is a victim mentality that will never get you what you want. If you're going to make changes, you have to take ownership of your past actions and the debt you have created. Only then can you take steps toward becoming financially free.

A SIMPLE APPROACH TO FINANCIAL FREEDOM

Getting control of your spending and achieving financial freedom (or financial independence, as some call it) requires a plan and a strategy. Hope is not a plan. You can hope that things will change, but hope will not make it happen. You need a plan.

I'll say it again: my approach to achieving financial freedom is simple, but it isn't easy. You will have to make hard choices and change your behavior.

So what does this approach involve?

- Before you can change your life, you need to change your mind. We'll talk about the difference between an abundance and scarcity mindset and the importance of feeding your mind on abundance and positivity.
- Next, I'll help you discover your big why: why do you want to get out of debt and be financially free? This chapter includes several questionnaires to help you determine your purpose. You will need to hang on to your big why when you get tired of delayed gratification and are tempted to splurge on something you really don't need or you really can't afford.
- After you've got your mindset straight and you know why you're making these changes, you need to get practical. I'll help you create a net worth sheet so you can see exactly where you are on your financial journey. Then I'll

share some tips for creating a budget to help control your spending, save money, and get out of debt. Finally, we'll figure out your financial freedom number—the amount you need to earn through passive income streams so you can live out your big why.

- The next few chapters discuss ways to fund your financial freedom number through passive income and small business ownership. We'll discuss real estate investments, dividend investments, and various side hustles. You have so many options for funding your freedom number, and the choice is yours!

Financial freedom is different for everyone. Some people need $2,000 a month in passive income to live the life they want, and others need $10,000 a month. Some people want the freedom to quit the job they hate and work in their passion. Others want the freedom to travel or spend time with family. Maybe you would love to volunteer. Financial freedom is a mindset and lifestyle, and the great news is that you decide what you want and how you're going to get there.

KENTUCKY GIRL BECOMES A MILLIONAIRE

At one point in my life, I was right where you are. I was in debt, and I needed to make some changes.

I'm from a rural town in Kentucky. I was raised by two loving parents who always reminded me that I could be or do anything I put my mind to. Mom and Dad were both school-teachers and they valued college education. They were not so keen when their youngest daughter announced she wasn't going to college. I wanted something different. I had dreams of being a self-employed hairstylist like my grandmother.

My family in 1970. I'm sitting on the floor in front of my mom.

My family in 2019. From the left, Milt, me, Mom, and Laura.

After graduation, when all my friends were heading off to college, I moved to Texas, the land of big hair. It was the perfect place for me to build my hair-cutting business. I worked two jobs while I attended Texas Barber College. At the ripe old age of twenty, I purchased a barber shop in the Northtown Mall in Dallas, Texas. My dad loaned me money for the down payment, and the barber who was retiring agreed to finance the rest.

I became a barber because I wanted to cut men's hair, but I quickly learned there was more money doing women's hair, so I started doing hair color, perms, and highlights. I worked seven days a week for the first few years. I went to the mall with my own big hair to solicit business. I offered people free haircuts, knowing that if I could get them in my chair, I would have clients for life. I earned a decent living on five-dollar haircuts and twenty-five-dollar perms (remember, this was the late '80s when Julia Roberts's spiral perm in *Pretty Woman* was all the rage!), and because I was so frugal, I saved at least half the money I brought home.

Then I got the news: my dad's lymphoma had returned and he was dying. My world turned upside-down. I started flying from Texas to Kentucky every weekend to help my mom take care of my dad. This meant I wasn't working on Friday and Saturday, my busiest days at the salon, and I was also spending a lot of money on plane tickets and other expenses. During a one-year period, I racked up over $10,000 in debt.

My dad passed away at just fifty-two years old, and it was such a huge loss. He was the pillar of our family and one of the most positive humans I knew. He never met a stranger and was loved by many. I can't talk about him today without crying. I know they say time heals all wounds, but it's been over thirty years, and the wound in my heart has never healed. I miss my daddy.

During the time my dad was sick, a friend introduced me to Rick Oliver, a policeman and avid pool player. It was love at first sight. When I pulled up to the pool hall with my friend, I could see inside through the big windows. "Just tell me he's the one in the red shirt shooting pool," I told my friend.

"That's him."

"I'm going to marry that guy." And I did, one year and three months later.

After my dad died, I started working to get out of debt. My whole life, I had watched my mom and dad struggle with finances. They both worked two jobs to make sure my brother, sister, and I had everything we wanted (but didn't necessarily need). What we really wanted, however, was to spend time with them. I knew that I did not want to work that hard and miss out on time with loved ones. So, over the next year, I focused on paying down my credit card debt and saving like crazy. In 1989, Rick and I were able to buy our first home.

A few years later, I had an aha moment: we could buy houses, rent them out, and build an income source. At that point, we had saved enough money to buy our first rental property for $18,000 cash, and by charging $400 a month for rent, we earned our money back in less than four years.

Around the same time, I read a book that was a real game changer. *Your Money or Your Life* by Vicki Robin and Joe Dominguez opened my eyes to what money could do for us if we were purposeful with it instead of wasteful. I started understanding the concept of trading time for money. I also started considering what we could do to earn passive income without trading time for money.

At the advice of one of my clients, I opened a retirement

account and started contributing to it every month. Rick and I also became more purposeful in saving money to buy rental properties and generate a bigger income stream. Our first goal was to earn $3,000 a month through passive income to replace Rick's salary so he could quit. By the time I was thirty-three, we had built a rental property portfolio of ten units that earned $5,000 a month.

With those rental properties, our retirement accounts, and other assets, our net worth was $1 million. We had done it! We were officially millionaires. My husband was able to walk away from the police department, I sold my hair salon, and we took a three-year sabbatical. We had reached financial freedom!

There were times when I wanted to go buy a new car or even a new outfit. There were days I was exhausted by saving my money. I saw other people spending like crazy at the mall, and I wanted to walk into those same stores like a soldier and say, "Charge!" We didn't like delayed gratification, but we knew if we stayed disciplined and consistent with our saving, we would be free, and we were right.

You have to be willing to do what others won't to get what others don't have. As you'll see, it's not how much money you make—it's how much money you keep and what you do with it. Keeping a lot takes sacrifice. You can have financial freedom if you take the simple approach laid out in this book. It's not easy, but it is simple.

Today, Rick and I have a life worth living, with freedom to do and go whenever we want. Being frugal in our twenties, thirties, and forties has given us the debt-free lifestyle we enjoy now. We have homes in Texas, Kentucky, and Florida, and we have a precious chihuahua named Izzy, who is probably at the platinum level with American Airlines because we don't go anywhere without our fur baby.

Our little girl, Izzy

If a hillbilly from Kentucky with a high school education can become financially free, so can you. This isn't a get-rich-quick scheme. It's not a lesson in playing the stock market. You will have to make hard choices. When the pain of staying the same is greater than the pain of change, then you'll make the change.

WHY I WROTE THIS BOOK

I thought that once I became a millionaire, my life would be perfect and I would be happy, but it didn't bring me the joy I expected. Within three years, I was back on the treadmill chasing more money and success. The thing is, I didn't need the money! Rick and I were debt-free, and our passive income covered all of our expenses plus some. But somehow, I was pulled back into the idea that power and success would give me happiness, and I was stressed and overworked as a result.

"Wait a minute," I said to myself one day. "Why am I still doing this?"

I made a list of things that bring me joy, and I realized none of them were money related. Yes, it takes money to buy certain things and to have the freedom to choose not to work. But it was the freedom I was into, not the money or power. I realized that time is finite and I was spending all mine at work instead of pursuing my passion.

So, on April 15, 2018, I quit the job that consumed my life and time. What I really wanted to do is make a difference in people's lives—people like you—so I decided to write a book to share what I've learned about financial freedom.

However, writing a book is very challenging! I'm a hairstylist turned real estate broker, not a writer. On one particular day,

I was struggling with what to say. I worried whether anyone would want to read it. With all new ventures comes doubt, and I was smack-dab in the middle of a pity party, filled with uncertainty, confusion, and scarcity.

As I pulled into my driveway that day, I saw this beautiful hawk sitting on my mailbox less than five feet away. It just stared at me. I rolled down my window and stared back.

Oh my gosh, I thought, *I need to get a picture of this! No one will ever believe this is happening.* I grabbed my iPhone and shot this picture.

As I pulled forward, a calmness came over me. The hawk flew over my car as I drove through the gates. I knew this was a sign, but I didn't know what it meant.

As soon as I got into the house, I googled, "What does it mean when you see a hawk?" One website said, "A hawk is a symbol of ability to be a leader in every situation. If this bird has crossed your path, it means that it is time to take initiative and lead other people."[2] I kept searching and found another article from PowerofPositivity.com. The whole article blew me away, but one line in particular stood out: "The hawk will help you gain confidence and realize that you have great potential to take initiative and see your goals and dreams through to the end."[3]

After reading that article, I knew I had just received the sign of encouragement I so desperately needed. Now, I'm on a mission. I've completed the journey of becoming a millionaire and achieving financial freedom. I'm proof that it can be done without a college degree, inheritance, or trust fund. Now I want to help others see their money and time differently. I want to inspire you to live your best life and become financially free.

Are you ready to change? Are you willing to delay gratification now so you can enjoy financial freedom later? In the pages that follow, I will show you the approach that worked for me. It can work for you, too.

Financial freedom is for everyone, and it's so worth it. So let's get started.

CHAPTER 1

————

Financial Freedom

"Rick, check this out! I found it!"

I was sitting on the living room floor, holding *The Dallas Morning News* classified ads and pointing to a three-bed, one-bath brick home for sale. "Let's go buy this house and make it a rental property!"

"Do you realize where that house is located?" Rick asked. According to my policeman husband, it was in a not-so-safe part of town.

"Everyone has to have a place to live. Let's buy it! Where else are we going to find a house for $18,000?"

I immediately called the agent, and we met him at the house about thirty minutes later. We wrote the offer right there on the spot, and within a month we had officially bought our first rental property and started our first passive income stream. Our journey to freedom had begun!

As a child, I had watched my parents struggle financially. They both had college educations, and in most people's minds, our family wasn't poor—being a schoolteacher in our rural part of Kentucky was a good job. However, trying to keep up with the Joneses gets very expensive and comes at a cost—most importantly, lost time together as a family. As a result, my parents were tied to their jobs and struggled to make ends meet.

I didn't want that. I didn't want to be tied to my chair cutting hair twelve to fourteen hours a day for the rest of my life. I wanted the option of working if I wanted to, not because I had to. I wanted to be free.

In this chapter, we'll talk about what financial freedom is and why we should pursue it. Financial freedom looks different for everyone, but given the current uncertainty around pensions and rising inflation, it is definitely something we should all strive for.

WHAT IS FINANCIAL FREEDOM?

So what is financial freedom? I define it like this: financial freedom is having enough passive income to pay for essential living expenses so you can work if you want to, not because you have to.

Financial freedom gives you options. It gives you the freedom to choose *if* you work, *where* you work, and *how much* you work. It gives you the option of working in your passion and not just for money.

Financial freedom also gives you peace of mind: You know you have enough money to pay the electric bill, mortgage, and health insurance premium. Or perhaps you have peace of mind knowing you don't have to make a mortgage payment at all because the house is paid for.

Financial freedom gives you the chance to make choices based on what you enjoy and whom you want to spend time with, rather than bills you have to pay.

How much money do you need to reach financial freedom? That number is different for everyone. It might be $3,000, $5,000, or $10,000 a month, depending on your expenses and lifestyle. The key is that you have enough to cover the essentials (housing, food, transportation, etc.) without being tied to a J-O-B. (You'll learn how to figure out your own "freedom number" in chapter 4.)

WHY PURSUE FINANCIAL FREEDOM?

When I was twelve years old, I knew I wanted financial freedom, although I wouldn't have called it that. I knew I wanted to be a millionaire and retire so I didn't have to spend my life working.

Most people plan for some level of financial freedom in retirement, after they reach the age of sixty-five or seventy. This is why people open individual retirement accounts and contribute to 401(k)s through their employer. Many people also plan on receiving Social Security benefits and pensions when they retire.

The problem is that these income streams are becoming less reliable. According to one article in the *Social Security Bulletin*, Social Security benefits are expected to be paid in full until 2037. At that point, the reserves will be exhausted, and people will most likely not receive the full benefits they're entitled to. The article says that after 2037, there will be enough money from ongoing taxes to pay 76 percent of the scheduled benefits.[4]

Even if people do receive their full Social Security benefits after 2037, the average check is $1,461 a month, which is hardly enough to live on. So, Social Security may be one stream of passive income, but it should not be your only retirement plan.

You also can't rely on employer-funded pensions to pay for your retirement. What happens if the company goes out of business? That retirement fund could disappear entirely or at least be drastically reduced.

This is what happened to my brother, Milt. He worked for the same company for twenty years and then found out that they filed Chapter 11 bankruptcy. As a result, the pension he had been counting on for retirement is going to be much smaller. Because Milt can no longer rely on this future income source, he's had to create his own passive income streams, and he decided to do that through real estate investments. (More on how he did this in chapter 5.)

There are two more reasons that you're better off building your own retirement fund through passive income streams: inflation and longevity.

INFLATION

Inflation refers to the general rise in prices for goods and services. It also refers to the decrease in the purchasing power of money; in other words, $10 or $1,000 doesn't buy as much as it used to.

The following table gives you an idea of how the average price for five essential, everyday expenses has increased between 1989 and 2018:[5]

	BREAD	MILK	GAS	CAR (NEW)	HOUSE
1989	$0.61	$2.30	$1.12	$12,000	$100,000
2018	$2.50	$3.50	$2.90	$35,285	$222,800

One concern related to inflation is that the price of goods and services is rising faster than incomes. According to the Census Bureau, the median US household income in 2018 was $63,179. That's an increase from $61,372 in 2017, or approximately 0.9 percent.[6] By comparison, the inflation rate for the same 2017–2018 time period was 2.49 percent.[7]

This is another reason to pursue financial freedom by creating your own passive income streams. If you don't take control of your money and your financial future, inflation is going to continually outpace your income and you might have to work many years longer than expected.

LONGEVITY

Another factor to consider is that we're living longer. Back in 1950, the average life span in the United States was sixty-eight. Because of medical improvements and the fact that we're generally taking better care of ourselves, the average life span is now closer to eighty.[8]

Living longer is wonderful, but it also means we have more years of expenses and we will need more money to pay for them. In addition, because of inflation, the cost of those expenses will continue to rise.

Think about it this way: if you live ten years longer than someone in the 1970s or '80s, you need ten more years of savings. Let's say you can live on $50,000 a year. If you live ten more years at $50,000 a year, you need another $500,000 saved up for retirement.

Where is that money going to come from?

As we've seen, pensions and Social Security alone are not a wise retirement plan. Your kids are not a good plan either. As some baby boomers have learned, you could end up taking care of your aging parents *and* your adult children. This is another reason why you need to pursue financial freedom and multiple streams of passive income.

TAKE CONTROL

We all need money to live, both now and in retirement. Why not make changes now so you can be free later to have your expenses covered while you enjoy life?

I can't imagine having to work a job for thirty years, day in and day out, just to pay the bills and then hope that the company stays in business so I get my pension. I don't want to hope that I'll get a Social Security check or that my employer will give me a raise so my income keeps pace with inflation. I want to control my financial future.

Every person on earth is going after the same thing: we all want happy, peaceful, fulfilling, purposeful lives. What's different about us is the everyday choices we make. It's often our small, daily decisions that cause us to struggle financially. If we keep our focus on financial freedom, we will make better choices day to day that will have a positive impact on our future.

Are you ready to take control of your finances? Do you want to be financially free? Then fire yourself today and leave all your ideas about money and finances at the door. If you're open-minded and willing to listen, I'm going to teach you how to think differently about money, and then you can rehire yourself as CEO of your life.

Pursuing financial freedom requires a mindset shift. You have to change the way you think before you can take action. As I've said, it's simple, but it's not easy. In the next chapter, we'll discuss how to change your mind so you can change your life.

CHAPTER 2

Change Your Mind, Change Your Life

For decades, track athletes tried to run a mile in less than four minutes, and no one succeeded. People started thinking it couldn't be done and that attempting to run a sub-four-minute mile could be deadly.

Then, on May 6, 1954, twenty-five-year-old Roger Bannister did the seemingly impossible. On the Iffley Road track in Oxford, England, Bannister ran the mile in 3 minutes 59.4 seconds.

Something interesting happened soon after: other athletes started breaking the four-minute barrier. Only forty-six days after Bannister set the record, an Australian runner ran the mile in 3 minutes 58 seconds. Three years after that, three runners ran a sub-four-minute mile in the same race.

We see this phenomenon in other areas, such as technology. There's some kind of physical or mental barrier, and as soon as someone breaks through, big things happen. All it takes is one person to lead the charge and show us what is possible. Afterward, people are no longer stifled. They are open to possibilities because they see it can be done.

We create situations and difficulties in our mind that just aren't true, but we believe they are. Your reality is framed by whatever your head is telling you. Whether you think you can or can't, you're right.

The mind is a powerful thing.

The good news is that you can control your mind. You can choose what to feed it, just like you choose what to feed your body. You can choose to live in abundance instead of scarcity.

In this chapter, we'll explore the differences between a scarcity mindset and an abundance mindset. We'll discuss ways to feed your mind on positive messages so you can live in abundance. If you're going to pursue and achieve financial freedom, you need to think big, and this is what an abundance mindset allows you to do.

Living in abundance instead of scarcity affects your whole life, not just your financial future. The great news is that you can choose abundance every day!

ABUNDANCE VERSUS SCARCITY

In 2015, my company decided to take the leaders to SEAL-FIT Training in San Diego, California, for a bonding experience. I thought I would die when my boss announced this. Up until that event, I had never worked out a day in my life! SEALFIT turned out to be a life-changing experience that showed me the power of the mind.

Every day, the instructors came screaming into our barracks at 2:00 a.m. We had to get dressed, put on our combat boots, and go outside for a mile run to the beach. Then we had to swim out into the freezing Pacific Ocean and tread water for thirty minutes, linked arm in arm as a team. One day, we had to walk in smaller teams carrying a heavy log across our shoulders. Man, did I have bruises the next day! Anytime someone didn't follow directions during that week or showed up late for an event, we had to drop to the ground and do push-ups until they told us to stop.

Me with Mark Divine, US Navy SEAL and founder of the SEALFIT training I attended. Mark has also written a book about the importance of mindset: *Unbeatable Mind: Forge Resiliency and Mental Toughness to Succeed at an Elite Level.*

The other people who participated were all physically fit. They kept expecting me to drop out. They all knew I didn't work out and wasn't prepared for this training, but I refused to quit. I just kept telling myself, "I can do this. I can do this.

I can do this." I decided I could do it, and I did. That week was so challenging yet so rewarding, and it really showed me how powerful my mind is.

"I can do this" thinking comes from a place of abundance. Like me, Roger Bannister lived in this mindset. He didn't buy into the idea that a sub-four-minute mile was impossible. He believed someone would break that barrier, and as he said in an interview, "I felt that I would prefer it to be me."[9]

Once you break through scarcity and live in abundance, all things are possible. As soon as Bannister unlocked the door to what was possible on the track, others dropped their scarcity mindset—their *stinkin' thinkin'*—and believed it was possible for them, too.

So what is abundance? What is scarcity? The following word pairs illustrate the difference between these two mindsets:

ABUNDANCE	SCARCITY
Positivity	Negativity
Faith	Doubt
Integrity	Dishonesty
Offense	Defense
Growth	Stagnation
Proactive	Reactive
Opportunity	Adversity
Confidence	Fear
Compassion	Indifference
Creative	Unimaginative
Collaboration	One-sided

As you can see from this list, abundance and scarcity are opposites. The abundance mindset is full of optimism and positivity, whereas scarcity is pessimistic and negative. People who live in abundance see and accept opportunity everywhere they look, but people who live in scarcity are averse to whatever comes their way. They don't attract opportunity; they shun it. They say no without even considering the option.

People with an abundance mindset like to collaborate and share ideas. They are positive and put out great energy. These are the happy ones! People who live in scarcity want to work alone. They don't collaborate in decision making; it's all one-sided. They are afraid of losing out—that someone will steal their ideas or they won't get credit. Abundant people are confident. They have faith that everything will work out for the best, whereas those who live in scarcity are always in doubt.

A person with an abundance mindset believes there is always more of everything in life, whether it's money, relationships, opportunities, success, or freedom. Someone with a scarcity mindset believes just the opposite. They live in fear, they are defensive, they are filled with resentment, and they are afraid of being taken advantage of in a way that causes them to lose money or time.

The abundance and scarcity mindsets show up in all areas of life, including the ways people relate to money and pursuing financial freedom.

People who live in *abundance*

- *live with an attitude of gratitude.* They appreciate the things they have, and they receive more as a result. I don't completely understand the energy at work here, but this is an amazing truth: when you're grateful for what you have, good things keep coming your way. Some people refer to this as the law of attraction, or the ability to attract into our lives whatever we focus on.
- *think win–win at all times.* They don't think the other person has to lose for them to win. They always think both sides are going to win.
- *believe the more you give, the more you get.* This is another

energy thing. People who live in abundance receive joy from giving, whether it's time, money, or effort. I get joy when I feel like I'm making a difference.

- *play the money game to win.* They're playing offense, looking for opportunities to save and grow their money. They search YouTube for side hustle ideas to increase income. They educate themselves on the stock market and other money-making strategies. They read books and blogs on how to make money with the money they have. People who live in abundance are always learning and growing, especially when it comes to the money game.

- *let their money work hard for them.* They keep their options open and look for ways to build passive income. People who live in abundance seek new ideas that allow them to work smarter, not harder, and that ultimately bring them to financial freedom.

On the other hand, people who live in *scarcity*

- *live with an attitude of ungratefulness.* They don't appreciate what they have, so they don't attract more. This is the law of attraction at work in the opposite direction. You get back what you put out, and people who live in scarcity and ungratefulness attract negativity. Then they blame others for their lack of money or things. They have a victim mentality, never taking responsibility for what happens.

- *think "I win" at all times.* Their attitude is, "We're going to do it my way or no way." In their mind, this is their world and we all get to live in it. People with a scarcity mindset fear that if the other person wins, they lose.

- *believe the more you give, the more it costs.* They look at giving as a huge sacrifice, because it takes away from what they have and what they feel they are entitled to. People with an abundant mindset, on the other hand, focus on the act of giving, not the cost.
- *play the money game so they don't lose.* They're so busy keeping their guard up that they're not going for the win. People who live in scarcity are constantly playing defense, and they miss opportunities to invest and have their money grow. Fear keeps them from taking chances.
- *work hard for their money.* They are protective of their money (or lack thereof). They don't keep their options open so money can flow. People who live in scarcity don't think outside the box and they're not collaborative or creative. They simply go to work every day as a reaction to the need to pay bills. That's the irony: they're working so hard for money, but they don't have time to enjoy that money because they're working so hard to get it.

Sometimes there's a reason people have a scarcity mindset—growing up poor, for example. My husband was raised by a single mother who struggled to support her family. At age thirteen, Rick started working to help his mom pay the rent. He didn't get to play sports in school because he had a job at such a young age. His mindset was shaped by his childhood experiences and having to worry about money so young.

When I married Rick, he still had this scarcity mindset. However, we are all shaped by our environments, and being around a positive person like me caused Rick to start seeing things differently. Now we live in abundance together.

Anyone can change their mind, but they have to want to.

HOW TO DEVELOP AN ABUNDANCE MINDSET

As we've said, the mind is powerful. It can make you or break you, not only in terms of achieving financial freedom but also in life. Like the athletes who believed the sub-four-minute mile was impossible, we can hold ourselves back because of our stinkin' thinkin'. Changing your mind truly is the way to change your life.

So how do you develop an abundant mindset? If you hang out with negative people, feed yourself negative messages, and dwell on negative thoughts, you're going to put out the same. However, if you wake up each morning and choose joy, if you hang out with positive people, if you feed your mind positive messages, you will spread the same positive energy. It's a daily choice, and it all begins in your mind. I choose joy every day in the following ways. Come join me!

FEED YOURSELF POSITIVE MESSAGES

If you feed your body only sugar and other unhealthy things, how do you feel? Not so good. If you feed your body vegetables and hit all the food groups, however, your energy improves and you generally feel better.

Your mind is no different. The scarcity mindset comes naturally, and it is reinforced by the negative circumstances in life: your alarm doesn't go off, you spill coffee in your lap on the way to work, your car breaks down, you lose your job… You get the picture.

To counteract the negative input we receive from circumstances, ourselves, and others, we need to consciously feed our minds positive philosophies and perspectives. Without positive input, our minds will naturally tend toward the negative. We will become personally depleted, and we won't have anything positive to give others.

Books and Podcasts

One way to counteract negativity is by reading books or listening to podcasts with a positive message. A few of my favorite authors are John Maxwell, Tony Robbins, Jim Rohn, and Zig Ziglar. These writers all communicate a message of hope. In various ways and in different words, they encourage readers with the idea that you have one life and *you* get to create it. If you're not happy with the life you're living, change it!

Here's a list of books to get you started:

- *Intentional Living: Choosing a Life That Matters* by John Maxwell
- *The Success Journey: The Process of Living Your Dreams* by John Maxwell
- *The 21 Irrefutable Laws of Leadership: Follow Them and People Will Follow You* by John Maxwell
- *Awaken the Giant Within: How to Take Immediate Control of Your Mental, Emotional, Physical, and Financial Destiny* by Tony Robbins
- *The 7 Strategies for Wealth & Happiness: Power Ideas from America's Foremost Business Philosopher* by Jim Rohn
- *Zig Ziglar's Life Lifters: Moments of Inspiration for Living Life Better* by Zig Ziglar
- *A Joy-Filled Life: Lessons from a Tenant Farmer's Daughter Who Became a CEO* by Mo Anderson
- *The Miracle Morning: The Not-So-Obvious Secret Guaranteed to Transform Your Life—Before 8AM* by Hal Elrod
- *Mindset: The New Psychology of Success* by Carol S. Dweck
- *The Energy Bus: 10 Rules to Fuel Your Life, Work, and Team with Positive Energy* by Jon Gordon
- *The Gifts of Imperfection: Let Go of Who You Think You're Supposed to Be and Embrace Who You Are* by Brené Brown

Reading books like these can change the way you see things, which will cause the things you see to change. Instead of seeing your glass as half-empty, you will start to see it as half-full or even overflowing.

I usually listen to audiobooks, but here are a couple of podcasts that have the same message of hope and positivity:

- *The John Maxwell Leadership Podcast*
- *Unbeatable Mind* podcast with Mark Divine

Daily Affirmations

Another trick is to create positive affirmations related to your particular weaknesses—the areas where you are prone to negative thoughts. For example, if you struggle with self-doubt or low self-esteem, you can create affirmations such as "I am good enough" or "I am the best version of myself today."

You can also use positive affirmations to remind yourself of your goals, particularly related to financial freedom. If you have a spending problem, for example, you can develop affirmations along the lines of "Today, I'm going to spend only $5 on lunch and that's it, because I am saving for my future" or "Today, I'm going to bring my lunch and put the $5 in my retirement account."

Early in my pursuit of financial freedom, I used a dry erase marker to write messages to myself on my mirror. Every day, I saw these positive affirmations: "I'm the best hairstylist," "I'm successful," and "I'm debt-free." It drove my husband crazy, but I needed to daily remind myself of who I was and where I was going. I recommend writing down your affirmations and placing them where you will look at them often.

In addition, try giving yourself a verbal pep talk when you look at your reflection in the mirror. I used to stand in front of my mirror and say, "I am a millionaire!" It might sound silly, but trust me, it works!

We all experience rejection and failure, which can have a negative impact on your mindset. If you feed yourself positive messages, you can keep moving forward in spite of these setbacks.

SURROUND YOURSELF WITH POSITIVE PEOPLE

Motivational speaker Jim Rohn once said we are the average of the five people we spend the most time with. He was referring to the fact that we are influenced by those closest to us, whether positively or negatively. These relationships affect every area of our lives—words, actions, choices, values, financial status, business success, and more.

If you spend most of your time with negative, depressed, unimaginative people, it will affect you. You will start thinking and acting like them. Knowing that we're already prone to negative and scarcity thinking, we need to spend time with positive people who fuel our energy and our joy.

Just as you can control your mind, you can control whom you spend time with. Find people you want to emulate, people you enjoy being around because of their bright attitude and their positive perspective on life. At the same time, you may have to limit time spent with those who drag you down. I've had to let people go out of my life because they were affecting my ability to live in abundance.

In his book *The 21 Irrefutable Laws of Leadership*, John Maxwell discusses the law of the lid. This law says that a person's lid to success in any area of life is set by those around him or her.[10] This includes the ability to live in abundance. If you surround yourself with negative, fear-driven, reactive people, you set the lid on how positive and confident you can be.

This law applies to your pursuit of financial freedom as well. If the five people you spend the most time with make

$25,000 a year, you're likely not going to make more than that. They've set the lid on your success. However, if you spend time with people who look for opportunities, think outside the box, and pursue passive income streams, you will do the same. The sky's the limit when you're with those people. You think bigger.

The law of attraction comes into play here as well. As you start living in abundance, you will attract others with similar thoughts, ideas, and goals.

WHAT TO DO WHEN YOU'RE STUCK

My abundant mindset got me where I am today, yet I still have days where I slip into scarcity. Everyone does. The key is knowing how to pull yourself out. You have to coach yourself back to abundance.

When I'm stuck in stinkin' thinkin', I phone a friend or listen to an audiobook by John Maxwell, Zig Ziglar, Tony Robbins, or Brené Brown. I also remind myself of the good things in my life. Thinking of something I'm grateful for is the quickest way back to abundance.

The first step is recognizing when you're thinking negatively. If you pay attention to what you think about and how you're thinking, you'll realize more quickly that you're stuck.

Next, get in the daily habit of thinking of things you're grateful for, because life will come at you daily. Negative circumstances will happen, and your mind will naturally shift into scarcity. When that happens, simply turn your mind back to something positive, something that brings you joy. Remember all the blessings you can be grateful for.

You can't bank big when you're thinking small. Thinking small comes from a scarcity mindset. Living in abundance allows you to believe the sky's the limit, which is what you need to pursue financial freedom.

Now that you understand the importance of living in abundance, you can take the next step on this freedom journey: figuring out your big why.

CHAPTER 3

Discover Your Big Why

After thirteen years of standing behind a chair ten to fourteen hours a day, I was done. I woke up one morning and told Rick, "I'm quitting."

"Go for it," he said.

I walked into my shop that day and approached my most loyal stylist. "Do you want to buy a hair salon?"

She laughed. "Of course!" She was in her fifties and I was thirty-three, but I was the one who was retiring. I financed her dream of owning a hair salon, and I got to live my dream of being financially free.

For the next three years, Rick and I bought rental properties, and I worked my network marketing business.

My first big why—my first reason for pursuing financial freedom—had been about buying back my time. Now that I was enjoying that freedom, however, I realized I was still missing something.

In 2001, I got my real estate license mainly because I wanted to buy properties and represent myself as an agent. Because of my work ethic, however, I quickly rose to the top in sales as an individual agent in my town. After ten years at an independent broker, I was approached about running the largest and most productive office in our town. So I became the Team Leader for Keller Williams Denton. I loved being able to share techniques and strategies with other agents to help them become successful. After three years as Team Leader, I was promoted to Regional Director for the Ohio Valley Region of Keller Williams Realty International, and I spent four and a half years in that role. During that time, we doubled the owner profit for our franchises and doubled the profit share for our agents. By all external standards, I was very successful.

In the process, however, I had slipped back into the trap of working twelve hours a day, seven days a week. I was again trading my time for money. Although I was making good money, I came to realize it wasn't giving me happiness. I felt like I was chasing someone else's dream. I became so consumed with success and winning the game that I wasn't even playing for myself anymore. I was not being true to myself and what I actually wanted out of life. So, in April 2018 at the height of my career, I resigned.

A few years earlier, I had attended a John Maxwell seminar where he said something I have never forgotten: "Success is great, but significance is where it's at." I had been pondering that statement ever since. When I quit in 2018, it all came together. I realized what was missing from my life: I wanted significance. I wanted to make a difference. I wanted to help people see what money can do for them and their family. That's how the Down Home Money platform and community were born. That's my new purpose, my big why.

You may struggle with discovering your big why. As you can see, I did. It didn't happen overnight, and it also changed over time. You might find the same is true for you.

Why do you get out of bed every day? What fuels your fire? What motivates you? This chapter will help you discover your big why and understand how it is fundamental to your pursuit of financial freedom.

KNOW YOURSELF

A person's big why is their purpose in life. It's what makes life worth living.

To discover your big why, you have to know who you are

and why you are the way you are. You have to understand what you like and don't like, what gives you joy, what you are passionate about, and what you value.

To learn these things about yourself, you have to be willing to sit and think. You have to pay attention to your thoughts and reactions and be present in your day-to-day life.

Asking yourself questions can help you gain this awareness. I've included three questionnaires to help you get to know yourself. If you take the time to answer each question honestly and thoughtfully, you will learn what gives you joy, what you value, how you view money, and what gives your life purpose and meaning.

THE JOY QUESTIONNAIRE

There's a difference between happiness and joy. Happiness is based on external people, places, and events, and it comes and goes. You might be over-the-moon happy one day because you got a new job, and then lose that happiness the next day because you get into a car accident. Joy, on the other hand, is an attitude or perspective on life that comes from within. Joy results from a peace with who you are and why you are. It is not dependent on external circumstances.

The following questions can help you think about joy and your experience of it:

1. How do you define *joy*?
2. On a scale of 1 to 10, how joyful are you?
3. What are the top five things that give you joy?
4. Describe how you feel when you are joyful.
5. What one thing can you do (or what one person can you be around) that always gives you joy?
6. If you could remove three things from your life or environment, with the result being more joy, what would they be?
7. Name three moments in your life when you felt overwhelming joy.
8. Do you consider your life being one of joy or sadness?
9. What steps can you take to have more joy in your life?
10. What one thing will you change today to have a more joyful life?

One of the things that gives me joy is my little chihuahua, Izzy. I am a huge animal lover, and I've had big dogs most of my life. Izzy is the first small dog I've been blessed with, and I have never felt unconditional love from a dog the way I do with Izzy. The way she sits in my lap, lays her head back on my chest, and looks at me just melts my heart. She makes me smile every single day. I love how Izzy sits in the front of her stroller on our walks, with her head out and ears back, taking it all in. Sometimes it's the smallest things in life that give you joy, and that is Izzy. She is my small bundle of joy!

Izzy, living her best life

We often have a hard time discovering what gives us joy because we don't stop long enough to think about it. See if this scenario sounds familiar: The alarm goes off at six o'clock in the morning. You get up, shower, dress, and drive the kids to school. By the time you get to work, you're ten minutes late. Your email inbox is full and your to-do list is a mile long. Suddenly, it's noon and you need to get something to eat but you don't have time to go outside, so you just eat at your desk. Then it's five o'clock. You pick up the kids and take them to ball practice. After practice, it's 7:30 p.m., and the kids are hungry, so you drive through McDonald's. At home, one of the kids asks for help on his homework, but now it's almost 9:00 p.m. and you're exhausted, so you fall into bed so you can wake up and do it all over again.

When this happens five days a week, week after week, when do you have time to figure out what you want and what gives you joy?

Start by carving out time to complete this joy questionnaire. It's time to slow down and declutter your mind so you can focus on being who you really want to be.

THE WEALTH QUESTIONNAIRE

In the dictionary, wealth is defined as "an abundance of valuable possessions or money." In my opinion, however, wealth differs for everyone; it is not necessarily tied to money or things. I see wealth as a choice you make in how you live your daily life. You can enjoy a wealthy life without having a lot of possessions and money.

The following questions can help you identify how you view

wealth, which will help you figure out what financial freedom will look like for you:

1. How do you describe wealth?
2. What do you need to have or own to think of yourself as wealthy?
3. Do you feel you are wealthy?
4. How would your life change if you were wealthy?
5. What are you willing to do or give up to start your journey to wealth?

THE PURPOSE QUESTIONNAIRE

According to the dictionary, purpose is "the reason for which something is done or created or for which something exists." For me, purpose involves the way you influence others. Discovering your purpose is crucial because it's what keeps you going when life gets hard.

The following questions can help you identify your purpose:

1. If you could do anything and you weren't limited by time, money, or location, what would you be doing right now?
2. What one thing fills you up every time you do it?
3. Why are you in the job you're in? (i.e., Are you making a difference? Are you working in your passion?)
4. What are you truly passionate about?

5. When you look back on your life, what do you want to be remembered by?

Most people don't take the time to think about these things. They don't plan their lives or consider what they really want out of it. By nature, we're creatures of habit, so we repeat the same actions and then complain about the outcome. This is the definition of insanity: doing the same thing over and over and expecting different results. It's time to stop the insanity by doing something different.

LIVING YOUR BIG WHY

Knowing your big why will positively influence your life in many ways. It will give meaning to your day-to-day life, help you stay focused on your goals, and give you clarity on the steps to get there. As you work toward something meaningful, you will become more joy filled and passionate.

MYRA'S MOMENT

How do you want to be remembered when you're gone? What is your legacy? What would you love that people felt about you? After you consider these questions, take some time to write out your own eulogy.

The good news is, you're still here! You get the chance to write your legacy every day. You get to choose what you leave behind and what you'll be remembered for. Why not decide now and make it happen!

THE 80/20 RULE

As you become more purposeful in living out your big why, you will likely find yourself more productive as well as more joyful. In the late 1800s, Vilfredo Pareto observed that life seems to work on an 80/20 principle: 80 percent of the outcomes (effects and consequences) come from 20 percent of the inputs (causes). Pareto made his observation in relation to wealth and population in Italy (e.g., 20 percent of the population owned 80 percent of the land; 20 percent of the population paid 80 percent of the taxes), but the principle can be seen in all areas of life. In my real estate office, for example, 20 percent of the agents produce 80 percent of the sales commissions.

We all have the same twenty-four hours in a day. Why do some people seem to get so much more done? Because they are purposeful with their time. They know what they want. They know their big why. If you work hard in your top 20 percent—that is, in your purpose and passion—you will work less overall and be more productive with the time you do work.

In addition, each of us has a top 20 percent activities or inputs that account for 80 percent of our joy and satisfaction. If you spend 80 percent of your time in your top 20 percent, you will be much more content. However, if you spend 80 percent of your time on things that don't matter or that don't bring you joy—cleaning house, mowing the lawn, doing your taxes—you will be less satisfied.

Your top 20 percent is your big why, your passion, your purpose. Find it, pursue it, and live in it, and you will find yourself working more effectively and experiencing more joy. It's just that simple.

YOUR REASON FOR SACRIFICING

Like everything else in life, living your big why requires money. Whether your big why is volunteering at animal shelters, working at a lower-paying job in your passion, donating to charitable cause, or helping your aging mom, you need money to fund your big why.

Some people work long hours at a job they don't like so they can live in their big why. Others work multiple jobs at night and on weekends. In this book, I'm offering a third way to fund your big why: financial freedom through passive income. In chapters 5–7, we'll discuss some passive income options in more detail.

However you fund your big why, you will need to make sacrifices. Knowing your big why will drive you forward when you have moments of scarcity and doubt. You will get tired of saving money and wonder if it's all worth it. There will be times when you want to go to the mall and buy everything in sight. If you know your big why, you will pause before you act. You will remember why you're doing this, how you're doing this, and what you will gain by doing this.

Until you figure out why you're pursuing financial freedom, your emotions will lead your actions. If you know your big why, however, you'll be led by facts. You'll know why you're working overtime, saving your money, delaying gratification, and not buying the new _____ (you fill in the blank). If you know your big why, you'll be motivated to do what you need to do.

Now you have your big why. You have taken time to sit, think, and ask yourself tough questions. You know the reason you're going to make hard choices and pursue financial freedom.

In the next chapter, things get real. We're going to find out where you stand financially so we can determine what you need to do to reach financial freedom.

CHAPTER 4

The Cost of Freedom

Have you ever made a New Year's resolution? Sure you have. If you're like me, you've probably resolved to lose weight, and after about a week, you go right back to your old eating habits.

Your resolution to achieve financial freedom is going to be different! This time, you're setting a goal *and* preparing your mind and heart before you start the journey. In addition, you'll have a plan to get there. After reading this chapter, you'll know exactly what you need to do to be successful.

This is where the rubber meets the road. Financial freedom is not about how much money you make; it's about how much you keep. How much you keep depends on how much you spend. In the following pages, we're going to figure out what you're spending your hard-earned money on and where you can cut back. Then we can use that information to determine your freedom number: the amount you need to earn through passive income to be financially free.

Are you ready? Let's get started!

KNOW WHERE YOU ARE

In the next sections, you have to be painfully honest with yourself. My hope is that you are so sick and tired of being sick and tired that you will make a commitment to do the process and that you will win big as a result.

LIST YOUR EXPENSES

Do you know how much you spend on a daily, weekly, and monthly basis? That's where this stage of the journey begins.

A great way to keep track of expenses is to get a small note-pad and write down every penny you spend. As I like to say, documentation beats conversation. By documenting your spending, you will internalize how much you're spending and what you're spending money on. Carry your notepad everywhere, and anytime you go to the movies or check out at the grocery store or pay a bill, write it down. The experts say it takes sixty-six days to form a new habit and have it become automatic,[11] so don't get discouraged if you forget now and then. Just get started!

For many people, listing expenses is the hardest part, but it is worth the effort. Achieving financial freedom is a marathon, not a sprint, and it starts with figuring out where you are right now. If you don't do this prep work, you won't have an accurate starting point for figuring out your financial freedom number later in the chapter.

If you're like most people, your biggest monthly expenses are housing, transportation, food, and insurance. Those are the easy ones to identify, but you have to think through the small expenses, too, because they really add up.

Here's a list to help you think through all the monthly expenses you might have:

- Mortgage or rent (if your insurance and property taxes are not included in your mortgage, add those to the list)
- Car payment or lease
- Food (groceries and eating out)
- Health insurance
- Car insurance

- Utilities (water, sewer, trash, gas, electric, cell phone, landline)
- Auto expenses (gas, repairs, parking)
- Other transportation (train, metro, light rail, bus)
- Cable television
- Internet
- Day care and babysitting
- School tuition (for your kids) or student loans (for you)
- Medical expenses (prescriptions, copayments, tests)
- House maintenance (landscaping, pool service, house cleaner, homeowners' association dues)
- Clothing and shoes (purchases, dry cleaning, laundromat)
- Pet expenses (grooming, veterinarian, food, toys)
- Recreation (gym membership, fitness classes, ski passes)
- Monthly memberships or subscriptions (Netflix, Hulu, Spotify, Apple Music, Sirius, Amazon Prime, YouTube Premium)
- Boat payment and insurance
- Motor home payment and insurance
- Vacation home expenses
- Vacations (air travel, hotels, rental cars, etc.)
- Miscellaneous (coffee, alcohol, cigarettes)
- Other credit card expenses

Even if you don't spend money on each item on a monthly basis (for example, you may not take a vacation every month), figure out what you spend each year and divide it by twelve. That will give you a monthly number.

EVALUATE YOUR SPENDING

Financial freedom comes in one of two ways:

1. Reduce your spending and expenses.
2. Make more money.

It's up to you which path you choose—or you can do both and get there faster!

We're going to begin with path number 1: reducing expenses. You just determined how much you spend each month. Now it's time to evaluate your spending and see where you can cut back.

First, find your last credit card statement and look at the charges. Do you have automatic payments for things you don't use? How about the gym you haven't been to in years? Or the subscription to the online newspaper you never read? Cut it out! Put down this book and cancel those memberships. If your gym membership is $40 a month and the newspaper is $10, you could be saving $600 a year right there.

Next, look for things you spend money on but really don't need, things like fast food restaurants, coffee shops, and snacks at the gas station. (Yes, this is going to be hard!)

A good starting goal is to cut 15 percent of your expenses. For example, if you spend $2,000 a month, you would need to cut $300 from your monthly expenses.

This may seem impossible, but think about it this way: if you drop the gym and newspaper, you've already cut $50 a month. Let's say you hit McDonald's three times a week and spend around $7 each time (or $21 a week), and you also drive through Starbucks every morning on your way to work for a grande soy latte with an extra shot ($4 each, or $20 a week). If you start brewing your own coffee and eating meals at home, you've just saved another $164 a month. That means you've already saved more than $200 with those four changes. You're well over halfway to cutting 15 percent. You can do this! You just have to get purposeful and make different choices. Remind yourself that the money you don't spend can be saved for building your future freedom and funding your big why.

Here are a few other ideas to help cut that 15 percent:

- Shop around for insurance: car, home, and health. People tend to stay with the same insurance company year after year, even when the premiums go up year after year. You might be able to save 10 percent a year just by switching insurance.
- When you go out to eat, have water instead of ordering a soda or alcohol. You'll save yourself at least $2.00 a meal—even more if you usually drink alcohol.
- When food shopping, buy off brands. I tested this at Walmart. A can of Ro-Tel diced tomatoes costs $0.95. A can of the same product in Walmart's Great Value

brand is $0.50 a can. Nestlé's creamer is $3.70, whereas the Great Value brand is $1.79. Lay's potato chips are $4.00 a bag. The Great Value bag is $1.50. On three items, I just saved $4.86. Imagine how that adds up to with a full shopping list over weeks, months, and years. (Honestly, I did not notice a difference in the way the two brands tasted either.)

- If you own your home and have a higher interest rate than what is currently available, look into refinancing. You will have some up-front costs, but these can be rolled into the mortgage, and a lower interest rate could save a lot of money in the long run. Ask your mortgage advisor if this option is right for you.

Your journey to financial freedom is all about taking control of your money so that your money doesn't control you. Start by cutting that 15 percent.

CREATE A BUDGET

Taking control of your money also involves creating a budget. Yep, I said it. You need a budget! If you're going to reduce spending and start saving toward financial freedom, you need a plan to allocate your money each month.

There is no such thing as a one-size-fits-all budget. Each person's budget will be different because each person has a unique combination of income and monthly expenses.

One thing that is true for everyone is that creating a budget doesn't have to be complicated. If you follow a few guidelines, making a budget is simple (though following it isn't always easy).

1. Don't spend more than you make. That's pretty self-explanatory. Your monthly expenses should not be greater than your monthly income.

2. Pay yourself first. That means set aside a certain amount for savings every month to go toward your reserves. Put saving in your budget. Your first goal should be one month's worth of living expenses, but work up to six months' worth of reserves. Most financial planners recommend saving 10 percent of your income, but 10 percent won't get you to financial freedom. Start with 10 percent and work toward saving as much as possible. People in the FIRE (Financial Independence, Retire Early) movement save up to 75 percent of their income so they reach financial freedom faster (I'll say more about FIRE in chapter 5). It's up to you. The more you save, the faster you get there. You get to decide!

3. Use the want-versus-need test. For example, is electricity for your home a want or a need? It's a need. Are water, sewage, and trash service wants or needs? Needs. Is a car a want or a need? It depends. If you live in a city that has public transportation, a car may be a want, not a need. Is cable a want or a need? It's a want. You can live without cable television (especially if you have internet), and if you're trying to cut back, that might be one expense you can do without, at least for a while.

If you're looking for a simple budget template to get you started, go to downhomemoney.com and click on the Money Tools tab. You can download the budget Excel spreadsheet and start filling in your numbers.

AVOID CONSUMERISM

Consumerism is a way of life in America. We spend money according to our wants instead of our needs. Consumerism is what leads us to buy a bigger house or a brand-new car or a fifth pair of running shoes even though we don't need it and can't afford it. Consumerism is the reason so many people are in debt.

It's time to see buying now, paying later for what it really is. When you use your credit card to buy things that you don't have money in the bank to pay for, you are making a choice to continue to work. You are choosing to spend your future income. If you don't have the money right now, that means you have to keep working to earn it. In three to five years, you might still be working to pay for something you buy today. This is a debt trap, and it's hard to escape.

Another problem with charging things you can't afford is that you pay interest on the unpaid balance month after month. That $200 jacket (which you couldn't afford in the first place) could end up costing you $300 or more by the time you pay it off. That's like throwing money away. It's time to learn the difference between wants and needs, to become purposeful about limiting your spending on wants, and to only buy what you can truly afford.

Pause for a moment and think about things you spend your hard-earned money on that you really don't need. Now think about how much time you have to spend at work to pay for those unnecessary things. If you don't like your job, that should really give you pause. You are delaying your own freedom by spending instead of saving. You are putting yourself in the position of having to stay at that miserable job to pay

---

MYRA'S MOMENT

To make it easier to document and track all of my expense documentation, I charge everything to my credit card. Then I pay off that card in full each month so I don't pay interest. I would not suggest using your credit card like this if you do not pay it in full every month.

for things you could really live without. Don't be a prisoner to your job!

It is one thing to go to work and sacrifice because you're building something, like financial freedom. It's another thing to have nothing to show for your hard work and sacrifice because you've spent every penny you earn—and more—on stuff you don't need. That is not a life worth living. I want to help you design your life so you don't live day to day and paycheck to paycheck.

When people work hard and come home tired, they often believe they deserve a reward for their effort. You know, like a treat: a night out at the movies or a new outfit or maybe a fancy expensive dinner. Does this sound familiar? Although you may hate your job and feel like you've earned something by making it through another day, this attitude of rewarding yourself now is delaying your financial freedom.

When you realize you're working a week and a half every month to make one payment on that new BMW, or that you're working a whole day to pay the interest on your credit card, you will start seeing things differently. You will become aware of what you spend, and you will start spending differently. Awareness is key to financial freedom.

When I was cutting hair and watching every penny I spent, I drove crappy little cars that Rick bought at auction. I drove one Honda hatchback that had only one seat for the driver, but I didn't care. The car did its one job: getting me from point A to point B.

DETERMINE YOUR NET WORTH

This next step is crucial. Determining your net worth will show you what all those years of working has given you so far.

Every year, I sit down on New Year's Eve and figure out my net worth and compare it with the previous year. It energizes me to start the New Year with a sense of pride at what I have accomplished, and it helps me focus on my goals for the year ahead. This may sound a little crazy right now, but once you see that needle moving toward wealth, you will be fired up to take action.

Here's how a net worth sheet works: Create a document that has two columns. Label the column on the left Assets and label the column on the right Liabilities. In the Assets column, list anything you own that has value: bank accounts, home, jewelry, vehicles, and so on. In the Liabilities column, list anything you owe money on: home mortgage, vehicle loan, credit cards debt, school loans, and so on. Include the amount each asset is worth (current value) and the amount owed on each liability. Then add up the two columns. The net worth equation is simple:

Assets – Liabilities = Net Worth

The following table shows you a completed net worth sheet. In this case, the value of the person's assets is greater than the amount owed on the liabilities, so the person has a positive net worth:

$369,500 (Assets) – $338,500 (Liabilities) = $31,000 (Positive Net Worth)

NET WORTH

ASSETS		LIABILITIES	
Asset	Value	Liability	Amount Owed
Home	$300,000	Home	$250,000
Automobile	$30,000	Automobile	$20,000
Boat	$20,000	Boat	$25,000
Jewelry	$3,000	Student loan	$30,000
Household	$10,000	Credit card	$12,000
Roth IRA	$6,000	Macy's card	$1,500
Checking account	$500		
TOTAL ASSETS	$369,500	TOTAL LIABILITIES	$338,500
TOTAL NET WORTH	**$31,000**		

If you are in your twenties, thirties, and maybe even early forties, your net worth might be a negative number. This is normal! You might still have student loans, automobile loans, or credit card debt. All of these liabilities negatively affect your net worth. Just know that it takes time to pay off debt, so don't get discouraged. If you start paying down these debts, your net worth will start increasing until it becomes a positive number.

You can create your own net worth sheet using this example, or visit downhomemoney.com and download the interactive template from the Money Tools section.

PAY DOWN DEBT

Once you have completed your net worth sheet, you will know exactly where you stand financially. The question is, do you have a positive or negative net worth? In other words, does the value of your assets exceed the amount you owe, or is it the other way around? Most people in their twenties and early thirties have a negative net worth because they have school loan debt and they're still early in their career.

However, if you have been working for twenty-plus years and your net worth is a negative number, that means you have worked for absolutely nothing up to this point. That might sound harsh, but sometimes you have to be knocked into reality. You have to be honest about where you are before you can move forward toward freedom.

If net worth is negative, how can you turn it around and start moving toward a positive net worth? By paying down debt.

Start with the loan that has the highest interest rate and pay it off. If you currently have a car payment, do one of two things: work on paying off the loan quickly, or sell the car and buy one you can afford without a loan. A car is a liability; it is not an asset. Cars depreciate quickly and they've become so expensive that it takes five to six years to pay them off, which is a huge burden on your monthly finances. Keep in mind that a car simply gets you where you need to go. You may want to ride in style but at what cost to your future self?

Next up, credit card debt. Credit cards have high interest rates. As mentioned earlier, if you don't pay the card in full each month, you get dinged with extra fees. One option is to look for a card that has a promotional special such as zero percent interest for twenty-one months, then transfer your debt to that card and pay it off at no interest. (You can check websites like CompareCards.com to look for low or no interest cards.) Think of all the money you'll save if you're not paying 17 percent on the balance each month! You have to be willing to do some work to look for resources and then take the time to make some changes, but the benefits are so worth it.

Another option is to go to your local bank and consolidate all of your credit card debt into one loan with a lower interest rate. Credit cards can be 17 percent and higher, whereas you might get a personal loan for 5 to 6 percent interest. You might even be able to include a student loan, which usually has a higher interest rate.

Financial freedom comes with a price. It takes consistency, transparency, diligence, and grit to keep going, but the goal line is in front of you and the reward is huge!

YOU CAN DO IT!

You will have days where you want to go spend money. This is normal. Simply remind yourself why you're cutting and saving. Money is infinite—you can always make more money—but you cannot make more time. You don't want to spend all your time working to pay for things you really don't need.

If you become focused and disciplined, getting out of debt and building savings can happen quicker than you think. The hardest part is getting started. Once you start seeing results, you will get addicted to saving money. To this day, I get a thrill from saving money. I love it! You will, too.

Beware: Your friends might make fun of you because you don't go out to eat as often because of your new saving habits. But ten years down the road when you're financially free and don't have to work while they're still living paycheck to paycheck, you'll have the last laugh.

There may be times when you need encouragement on this journey. You can subscribe to blog, vlogs, or websites that give wealth-building tips and strategies. You can start with mine at downhomemoney.com. You might also read books like *The Millionaire Next Door* by Thomas Stanley or the updated version, *The Next Millionaire Next Door*, which Stanley wrote with his daughter Sarah Stanley Fallaw. The first book gave me hope while I was on my financial freedom journey, but it was written in 1996, so you might read the 2018 edition instead. Some people think the only way to wealth is by earning it. Stanley shows this isn't true. He explains how ordinary people, many of whom are blue-collar workers, became millionaires through saving.

Anyone can save money. Anyone can spend thirty minutes looking for credit cards with lower interest rates. Anyone can approach their local bank about a loan to consolidate debt at a lower interest rate. Financial freedom is an opportunity that does not discriminate. However, not everyone will take the opportunity because delayed gratification is a huge part of this journey, and it's hard.

You can design your future, and it starts with taking control of your spending, saving your money, and paying down debt. You can do this!

KNOW YOUR FREEDOM NUMBER

Now let's talk about your freedom number: the amount of money you need to earn from passive income to cover all of your monthly expenses without having to work. It's the number that will set you free from being a prisoner to your paycheck.

YOUR NUMBER MAY CHANGE

Your first freedom number comes from the monthly expenses total you identified earlier in the chapter, before you cut 15 percent of your expenses and before you paid off debt. That's your first goal.

This number will most likely change over time. It may go up or down for a variety of reasons. For example, if you get serious about paying off debt, you will lower your monthly expenses total and thus you can lower your freedom number. Or you may decide to quit the job you hate because you would rather make serious cutbacks than spend another day trading time for money. If you can live on less—by downsizing your house, selling your car and buying one without a car payment, eating at home, and so on—you can significantly lower your monthly expenses and your freedom number.

On the other hand, as time passes, you will likely experience life situations that cause an increase in monthly expenses, and thus in your freedom number: inflation, illness, a new child, desire for more space, a family member needing help.

The good news is that you are not a tree; you are not planted. You can move your financial freedom number up and down as needed. Just keep in mind that the bigger the freedom number, the more you will need to work to build passive income streams to cover that number. You can build a passive income portfolio to throw off $3,000 worth of monthly expenses faster than you can cover $5,000 in expenses.

How badly do you want financial freedom? How badly do you want to quit that job? That's what will determine how quickly you reach your freedom number. Your pursuit of financial freedom is largely based on your commitment to being frugal and delaying gratification.

FINANCIAL FREEDOM IS DIFFERENT FOR EVERYONE

Everyone has their own freedom number, based on their

necessary expenses, their lifestyle choices, and their big why. Some people can get by with $2,000 a month; others need $10,000. The great news is that you get to decide, understanding that the higher your number, the longer it will take to cover it and the more money you will need through passive income to set yourself free.

For some people, financial freedom is about living debt-free; it's not about quitting their job. They want to keep working because they love what they do and they experience growth there. For others, financial freedom means not working at all. They want the freedom to sit at home, watch TV, sleep late, and eat bonbons all day. Because financial freedom is so personal, you must each figure out your own big why and what you want out of life. Then you can set your freedom number and start working to fund it.

FUND YOUR FREEDOM NUMBER

Now you know where you are financially and you know how much you need to cover your expenses and be financially free. The next question is, how are you going to get there? Remember, there are two ways to achieve financial freedom: reduce spending or make more money or do both. Cutting back on spending and paying down debt is a good start, but to have the freedom to not work, you need a passive income stream to replace your current salary.

The next three chapters discuss options for building passive income: real estate investments, dividends, and small business ownership. Which path you start with partly depends on your current financial situation.

Before you read further, do a little self-evaluation. If you have paid down debt and are saving a little each month, you're ready for chapter 5 on real estate investments. This is a great place to learn how to turn your savings into real estate assets that bring in passive income.

If you are still debt ridden and living paycheck to paycheck, your first step is to make more money; chapter 7 on side hustles and small businesses will give you several ideas. Before you start investing, you need to earn enough money to cover your expenses and have a little extra. After you've increased your income and have some savings, come back to chapters 5 and 6 for ideas on how to invest and build your passive income streams.

No matter which chapter you choose, give yourself a little pat on the back at this point. The fact that you're reading this book means you have taken the first step to freedom. Congratulations!

Now it's time to get serious. Don't let debt and consumerism control your life. Take back your life and start building a passive income. You got this!

CHAPTER 5

———

Real Estate Investments

When I was growing up, my mom always used to say, "Where there's a will, there's a way." I believe there's a lot of truth to that statement, and I believed it even more after an incident involving our first rental property.

Rick was at the house replacing the wood floor. He had the doors wide open because it was summer in Texas, and he was saving money by not turning on the AC. He looked up from his work as a small Hispanic woman walked in.

"Can I help you?" Rick asked.

"Holá," the woman began and then kept talking in Spanish.

Rick understood enough to realize the woman was asking if

the house was for sale, not for rent. To the best of his ability, Rick explained that the house was not for sale and that he did not speak Spanish. The woman smiled and left.

A few hours later she came back with her nineteen-year-old son, who spoke English.

"My mom wants to buy your house. She has cash," he explained as he pointed to the paper bag in his mom's hands. The woman opened the bag and showed Rick the money—around $25,000!

Rick was shocked, to say the least, and as a policeman, he was very concerned that they were carrying around a bag full of money!

"I'm sorry, but we're getting the house ready to rent," Rick told the son. "If we do decide to sell, we will do it the correct way and go to the title company and close."

Later that day, Rick came home and told me the story. I was amazed, first that they showed up with a bag of money, and second that this woman was so determined to buy our house.

Rick and I talked it over and decided we could sell the house to this woman and reinvest the profit in a rental property closer to us. Rick had to drive an hour each way to take care of this property, and he was getting tired of it. We negotiated with the woman's son and made it happen.

After we closed the deal, the son told us what his mom had gone through. As a single mom who spoke no English, she had moved to the United States and earned money by ironing clothes for people at twenty-five cents an item. She kept working and saving until she had enough to pay cash for a house, which she turned into a rental property. Then she started saving the money from rent, along with the money earned ironing clothes. When she had enough to buy another house, she did and turned that into a rental property as well. Besides our house, she had purchased three other houses in the neighborhood—all cash. Like my mom said, where there's a will, there's a way.

In this chapter, we will discuss how to build passive income through real estate investment. I'll give you basic strategies for getting started, as well as tips and tricks that have worked for me and others. You'll also hear first-person stories from ordinary people who started investing in real estate in their twenties and were financially free in their thirties.

I guarantee there will be times when you slip into stinkin' thinkin' and doubt you can do this. When that happens, remember the woman who showed up at our house with a bag of money. If she could come to this country not knowing the language and work hard enough to buy four properties while making twenty-five cents a shirt, you can build a rental portfolio, too.

JUMP IN!

To me, real estate is the perfect place to start building passive income stream, although it does require a little money up front. If you're still living paycheck to paycheck, chapter 7 gives you some ideas for increasing your income so you can save up to buy your first rental property.

For the most part, generating positive cash flow from real estate takes less time than it does from dividends and stock investments. Plus, building a decent passive income from dividends requires much more money up front. That doesn't mean you shouldn't invest in stocks and index funds; you should start that immediately if you have a 401(k) or any other retirement plan (and be sure to max it out, especially when your employer is matching; more on retirement accounts in chapter 6).

With real estate, you can save enough for a down payment to buy a house that you can immediately start renting for positive cash flow. For example, if a property costs $100,000, a 5 percent down payment is $5,000. Let's say you charge $1,000 a month in rent, so you're immediately earning $1,000 a month on your $5,000 investment. That's $12,000 annual gross income! (Of course, you still have to pay mortgage, taxes, insurance, and repairs, so your net income will be lower.) An investment portfolio of $5,000 will not earn that kind of return. In fact, my $6,765 investment in AT&T stock earned me $104 in dividend income in the second quarter of 2020—that's only $416 annually. Compare that with $12,000 earned from a $5,000 investment in real estate!

Still, the thought of jumping in might make you nervous, especially if you're still renting and haven't bought your first house yet. Fear (false evidence appearing real) is powerful and it can hold you back from doing great things. Don't let that happen! As discussed in chapter 2, you can control your mind, and this chapter will give you practical steps to follow in building a rental portfolio.

Buying your first rental property will be the hardest and will take the most time, but this is true of almost everything when you first start. You will learn as you earn, and the end result will be so worth it.

We bought our first house in 1989 for $35,000. In 1994, we moved out and started renting that house. Over the last twenty-six years, we have earned over $300,000 in rent from that house alone, which we have used to buy more properties, from which we collect more rent. Plus, the house itself is now valued at $175,000, and we own it free and clear. I would say we made a good investment—especially since the tenants actually paid for the house!

Me standing in front of our first house more than thirty years after we bought it.

Our first rental property was the one I found when I was sitting on our living room floor looking through the newspaper. We paid $18,000 cash and we rented that house for $400 a month. Because we paid cash, we didn't have a mortgage, so the $400 was mostly profit (minus maintenance expenses, property taxes, and homeowners insurance). Within four years, we had earned back our initial investment. That gave us a taste for what's possible.

Our next goal was to own three properties within three years; we ended up having five properties. I kept working long hours at the salon and saving my income and tips so we could buy more rentals. Our first freedom number—and honestly the hardest number to hit—was $3,000 a month so Rick could quit the police department. Once we hit that goal, we moved the goalpost to $5,000 a month so I could quit working as well. Over the years, we moved our freedom number again and again. Today, we bring in more monthly income from our rental portfolio than most people make in a year. I don't say this to impress you but to show you what is possible. There's nothing special about us. Yes, we sacrificed and saved, but you can do the same. Today, we enjoy freedom because we were willing to work hard and delay gratification for a decade. We no longer trade our time for money. Are you willing to work hard for ten to fifteen years to never have to work again?

Some of you may be thinking, *Well, that was easy for you. You paid $18,000 for your first rental. Houses aren't that cheap anymore!*

I have some great news for you: cheap houses are out there! In 2019, I interviewed Heather, who had recently bought a house for $15,000 in Cincinnati; you'll read Heather's story later in this chapter. You'll also read about my brother, Milt, who lives in Kentucky and bought four rental properties in 2019 at prices ranging from $22,000 to $49,000. Houses under $50,000 are available across the country, but you have to look for them. If you live in an expensive city like San Diego or Seattle, you may need to look for rentals outside of the area where you reside. In fact, if your area is outrageously expensive, you may need to evaluate whether you should continue living there. Can you live on a lot less in a different city? Moving to a less expensive city is a choice you might need to make in your pursuit of financial freedom. By lowering major monthly expenses such as a mortgage, you can knock off several years of saving and reach freedom faster.

In preparation for writing this book, I interviewed several people who own multiple rental properties. When I asked for one tip they would give someone who is thinking about buying their first property, they all said the same thing: jump in as soon as possible.

I agree. Sometimes you will feel like you're drowning, but you will learn to swim. Nothing in life is easy, but investing in rental properties will be worth it. The rewards will be financial freedom.

TIPS AND TRICKS

This section will walk you through the big steps in purchasing your first rental property. I'll share strategies that have worked for me, and you'll also hear from two more individuals who reached financial freedom in their thirties through real estate investment.

START SAVING

First things first: If you don't have money saved for a down payment or to pay cash, that's the place to start.

How much should you save? The goal is to save enough to pay 20 percent of the purchase price as a down payment. If you put down less than 20 percent, you will be required to pay private mortgage insurance (PMI) along with your monthly mortgage. However, if the property will provide enough cash flow to cover PMI, you might want to do a smaller down payment, say 5 percent, to get into the rental market and start earning passive income (we'll see how this was done in Nick's story later in this chapter).

MYRA'S MOMENT

One reason our monthly income increased so significantly is that we paid off our rentals as soon as possible. Every time we received rent, we made an extra payment on the loan principal. Of course, we still pay for insurance, taxes, and repairs, but with no monthly mortgage, we have a much larger cash flow per property. If you follow the same strategy, you won't need as many properties to provide a passive income that throws off your freedom number.

CHRIS'S STORY: FROM POVERTY TO FINANCIAL INDEPENDENCE

I bought my first house when I was twenty-three years old. The circumstances regarding the purchase were bittersweet. The property had been the family home for the last ten years. My mom had passed away six months after her cancer diagnosis, and the home had been left to my brothers and me.

During college, my finance professor had encouraged us to purchase a home due to the current inflationary pressures, so I decided to heed his recommendation and bought the house from my brothers. It was a small three-bedroom, one-bath house with about 1,100 square feet, including a garage conversion.

Buying my first home was surreal, given that just ten years prior, when I was thirteen years old, our family had been homeless due to a domestic violence situation. For a couple of days, I lived in a station wagon at the lake with my mom, three brothers, and a couple of dogs. Money was scarce, and we boys had to work to help pay the family expenses.

My second purchase was a lot near the university that was about one-third of an acre and had two single-family homes. I bought it from my high school geometry teacher. He knew I had an interest in real estate investing and decided to sell me the property. The financing was secured by three owner-financed loans, which allowed me to purchase the property with very little money out of pocket.

Over the next few years, I purchased a couple of homes while pursuing my master's degree in counseling and student services and working full time as a computer programmer. I managed all my own properties but contracted out the maintenance and repairs.

After working as a computer programmer for five years, I realized I was working hard to help someone else achieve financial independence. If I was going to work hard, I wanted it to help me become financially independent! I quit my job and began selling real estate.

It was a huge risk. I did not want to be poor again. I made virtually no money my first year and thought I had made the biggest mistake of my life. However, I stuck with it and was able to create opportunities for income and investments.

The real estate crash of the late 1980s and early '90s was a game changer for me. I realized by that time the tenants were paying off the debt on my properties, a forced savings account you could say. Each time I made a mortgage payment, it was like someone depositing the equivalent of the principal part of the payment into a savings account, which meant more equity in the property for me. I went on a buying spree. Over the next twenty-four months, I bought eight townhomes, several houses, and a fourplex. I used my real estate commissions and the sale of a couple of properties to purchase the additional real estate.

I became financially independent when I was thirty-five. What I mean by financially independent is the income from the properties were sufficient to pay my living expenses. I did not need to work another job to cover my bills.

Over the next few years, I worked at buying, selling, and remodeling properties. I also decided to attend law school. The cash flow from my properties allowed me to self-fund my law school education together with my living expenses.

Even though I was financially independent, I needed to raise capital to expand my portfolio. Therefore, I created a plan to sell the oldest properties to provide the capital to purchase additional ones. The oldest had the most equity. I typically do not flip properties because I do not need the cash and I want to own them for a while so others can pay off the debt.

To generate additional capital for investments, I decided to sell my townhomes. I had purchased the townhomes for the average price of $35,000 each. I found a buyer who was willing to pay about half a million dollars for all eight townhomes. The check at closing was the largest I had ever received, around $400,000. Most of the townhomes were paid off at the time of closing.

Selling the townhomes allowed me to go to the next level of investing.

Using the proceeds from the sale of the townhomes, I purchased two homes with a friend of mine and my first small apartment complex. It was a twelve-unit complex near the local university. I was able to get the owner to finance the note with 20 percent down.

I gutted the apartment building. I replaced all the windows, doors, and balcony railings and added additional balcony overhangs. I held that property for about ten years and sold it for more than 2.5 times what I'd paid. The property was paid off at the time of the sale. Again, paid off by someone else!

The two homes I purchased with my friend were traded for a ten-unit apartment complex near the university. We used the equity from the ten-unit to purchase another twelve-unit near the university. We sold both of those properties about eight years later for more than twice the original purchase price. Again, the properties were almost debt-free, paid off by someone else. What began as two rental houses using only $8,000 became twenty-two units netting almost $990,000 for each of us. (A note of caution: If you decide to have a partner, choose wisely. Your worst deal may not be the property purchased but the partner chosen.)

I have been financially independent for over twenty years. The stories described are but a sampling of my real estate activity. My portfolio has continued to grow. I now have an assistant who helps with bookkeeping and a wonderful group of contractors for remodeling. (Tip: Treat your contractors well. They are a key factor in the success of your business.)

A few closing thoughts. Start small. Time is your friend. Time can turn a mediocre deal into a good deal through equity appreciation and debt reduction. Invest pursuant to your risk tolerance. If you feel uneasy about a particular deal, listen to your instincts. There is a fine line between the fear of taking a risk and intuition that says, "Walk away." Know the difference.

You are in the people business when you own investment real estate. Treat people as you would want to be treated.

Financial independence allowed me to serve my community as an elected official for over twelve years, six as Mayor. Pay it forward. If a boy from an economically challenged family who was once homeless can achieve financial independence, so can you.

Lastly, I thank God for my blessings. Without God's grace and love, I would not be in the place I am.

Keep contributing to this savings account after you buy your first rental. Your goal is to build up enough reserves to cover three months of expenses for each rental. If a tenant moves out or stops paying rent, you still have to pay your mortgage, so building this reserve fund is a crucial step in building a successful rental business. You should also keep saving for your next rental purchase.

GET PRE-APPROVED

Get into a relationship with a banker or mortgage lender and get prequalified for a loan. That way, you'll know what you can afford before you start shopping. You'll also know how much you need to save for your down payment and closing costs.

If you can't get prequalified—for example, if your credit is still recovering from past financial choices—you may need to put buying rental property on hold. In the meantime, build up your savings account with consistent monthly deposits so you'll be ready once your credit is repaired. Eventually, you will get there. If you don't start now, you may never get started, so take action one way or the other.

HIRE A REAL ESTATE AGENT WITH A RENTAL PORTFOLIO

Aside from saving for a down payment, this is the most important thing you can do when you start buying rental property. Hire a great agent who has years of experience and who owns rental property in the area where you want to buy. There is no better teacher than someone who has experience, someone who can share the good, bad, and the ugly.

How do you find an excellent, trustworthy agent? Call around and ask about agents who specialize in investment property. Don't hire the first agent you interview. Don't accept whoever has the listing for the property. Look for a buyer's agent who owns properties and will represent you, teach you, and help you through the process.

When you interview potential agents, ask the following questions:

- Do you own rental property in this area?
- How long have you owned rental property?
- Do you have a list of contractors to share with me?

A real estate agent with rental property will have contacts for maintenance and other professional services. You will want to shop around to find the best professional at the best price, and your agent can help you get started.

KNOW YOUR BOTTOM LINE

Most investors I talk with know exactly what their bottom line is—that is, how much profit makes a rental property a good investment. The amount is different for everyone.

When Rick and I started our rental property portfolio, we needed to make at least $200 to $300 net profit after all expenses (maintenance, loan payment, property taxes, homeowners insurance). Our strategy was to pay cash for cheap houses so they would immediately be cash positive. With no loan, most of the rent was net profit (minus insurance, maintenance, and taxes). We bought one rental for $16,000 cash and rented it out for $500 a month. In one year, we made $6,000 in rent, and the house had paid for itself in three years.

Now we have a 1 percent rule: we have to be able to rent the property for at least 1 percent of the purchase price. For example, if we're going to pay $100,000 for a house, we want to be able to rent it for at least $1,000 a month. If I'm driving around a neighborhood and I'm not sure what houses are renting for, I'll call on For Rent signs to find out (I often end up talking to the owner, which has even led to me buying the house!).

My friend Randy has a simple formula when he's evaluating

whether or not to buy a property. He figures his monthly expenses on the house minus what he could charge for rent. If he can make $300 to $400 a month in net profit, he buys it. It's that simple.

Randy started investing and buying property when he was in his mid-twenties. In college, he had worked for his uncle, mowing lawns and collecting rent on his uncle's five properties. After that experience, Randy knew he wanted to be the guy who owned the properties, not the one working on them.

Randy started saving his money and bought his first property a few years after he graduated. By the time he was thirty, Randy owned four properties. Now in his mid-forties, Randy owns thirty-one rental properties, a few of which are paid off.

Believe it or not, great deals are still out there; you just have to look for them. They may not be in the most desirable neighborhoods, but you can be the spark that helps revitalize the area if you buy a home and fix it up to be the nicest one on the block.

HAVE YOUR AGENT SET UP A SEARCH

Real estate agents can set up search parameters so you receive info on all the houses that meet your criteria. Your search should include things like location, price, and property features such as age of the house and number of bedrooms and bathrooms.

Seasoned investors have different criteria for the kind of rental properties they look for. Randy looks for single-family homes, and he prefers For Sale by Owner. Chris, on the other hand, looked for apartments as well as single-family homes.

Over the years, Rick and I have developed our own list of criteria. For example, we look for houses that are within thirty minutes of where we live because Rick takes care of the maintenance. We've also learned that tenants stay longer in houses than they do in apartments, which means less time and money making it ready for the next tenant. As a result, we focus on single-family homes. In general, we steer away from condos because of the dues, which cut into your income capacity. Plus, you never know when there's going to be a random HOA assessment on top of the condo fees.

You'll develop your own list of criteria over time, but here's our list to get you started:

Bedrooms and Bathrooms

We look for minimum of three bedrooms and two bathrooms. The more bedrooms and bathrooms a house has, the higher rent you can charge because people can get roommates to share the cost. We like houses with two or more bathrooms because they rent quicker than houses with one bathroom. The quicker you can re-rent a house, the better. Otherwise, you might have to pull from your reserves to pay the mortgage when no one is paying you rent.

Age

When we started building our rental portfolio, we bought older, cheaper properties, because that was what we could afford. Now we prefer houses that are twenty years old or newer. In general, newer houses have fewer maintenance issues. We are currently reworking our rental portfolio to sell some of our older properties and invest in newer ones. The key is to just get started, which might mean buying older houses for a while.

Style

We like the old frame-style houses that have crawl spaces because it's easier to move the plumbing if you decide to remodel or make repairs. In Texas, most newer homes are built on slab foundations, so that's what we're buying now.

HOA

Be careful of neighborhoods with an HOA (homeowners association). Some have written rules against certain types of rental properties. I found that out the hard way. I sold a property to a client, and then I helped him rent it out to four college kids. It's a college town, so this isn't uncommon. A neighbor complained, and the boys were forced to move out because the HOA didn't allow renting to nonfamily members or roommates.

With HOAs, you can also receive unexpected assessments that cut into your annual profit. Let's say it's time to paint the 700-unit condo project, but painting is not in the HOA budget. The HOA will divide the cost among the owners, including you. In 2019, I owed an additional $4,000 because of one of these assessments—the HOA was putting in new wooden stairs.

In addition, you may receive a lot of warning letters if your tenants don't follow the HOA guidelines regarding lawn mowing, watering, and taking in the trashcans.

Price

We prefer cheaper homes, in the $50,000 to $150,000 range. Given our 1 percent rule related to our bottom line, we want to charge at least $1,500 for a house we pay $150,000 for, and that's hard to do in our area. Once you go over $1,500, renters are harder to find and houses tend to stay on the market longer. The faster you can rent, the better because the longer the house is vacant between tenants, the more money you lose.

Miscellaneous

We look for established neighborhoods and good schools. We also take note of the houses on either side of the property we're considering. For rental income to stay up, it's crucial that you don't have unkept houses around you. People will judge your property by the ones around it, and they may not be willing to pay what is actually a fair rental price for your house.

In addition, unkept houses with multiple cars parked in the yard means they probably have way too many people living in the house. This makes it hard to attract good renters. Keep in mind, if the neighbors have roach and mice problems, those critters can easily infest your rental property as well. Always ask yourself, Would I live here?

We look for properties that have all electric appliances, rather than gas and electric, so tenants have only one monthly utility bill instead of two. We also prefer central heating and air because they seem to bring in more rent than houses with window units.

DO YOUR DUE DILIGENCE

Before you buy any property, you need to do your due diligence and make sure you're buying a good investment and not a money pit.

Inspections

When you buy your first rental property in particular, you don't want to buy something that is going to drain your funds. Be diligent with inspections. Remember, you are a novice, and you need all the advice you can get. This is another reason to hire a real estate agent who owns rental property. He or she can help you understand the inspection report so you can ask the inspector all the right questions.

The inspector knows a little about everything. If he or she guides you to hire a professional to check something more thoroughly, do it. If the inspector recommends that you have the air conditioner checked further, hire a licensed professional to do the inspection. You cannot be too safe on your first property. It can make or break you in the rental business.

It is better to spend money on the front end and know exactly what you're getting into than to find out later when you're in a financial bind over repairs that you could have had the seller take care of before closing the sale.

Get a Home Service Contract/Home Warranty

I always advise clients to ask the seller to pay for a home service contract. If the seller refuses, you should consider buying one yourself. The home service contract, or home warranty, usually costs $400 to $600 for a year and covers most major systems in your home, such as the air conditioner, as well as plumbing and regular appliances (refrigerator, stove, dishwasher, etc.). If the air conditioner goes out, for example, you pay the service charge (usually between $50 and $100) and the unit will be replaced or repaired. Without the home warranty, a new AC could cost you $5,000. I consider home warranties essential for the first year you own a rental property, while you are learning the ropes and building up your reserves.

Your agent can give you information on which home warranty companies are credible. Different companies operate in different states, and some companies are definitely better than others. Your agent can help you navigate this decision.

Know the Rental Market

Know the rental market and the lease terms for that area. One way to learn the market is to drive around neighborhoods, look for For Rent signs, and call to find out what other landlords are charging. I also suggest you start taking a landlord to lunch once a month so you can pick their brain. Find out how they got started, what they've learned, and what they consider best practices. Continue this practice after you become a landlord so you can compare notes with others. Knowledge is power, so talk to as many like-minded people as you can, whether their rental properties are commercial, homes, duplexes, or condos. You won't know it all when you start, but you will learn while you earn. I look forward to that invitation to lunch!

TIPS FROM PEOPLE WHO HAVE DONE IT

I interviewed several people who started buying rental properties when they were in their twenties and thirties. Here are some of their top tips:

- Find someone to look up to who has rental property and ask questions.

- Do your homework and be diligent about inspections, especially on your first property. That first house can make or break people in rental property. This is where having a real estate agent who knows and owns rental properties is crucial. There's nothing worse than buying a bad property right off the bat. If you lose money when you sell it, that'll discourage you from ever buying another rental property.

- You're going to lose money at some point. You're going to make a mistake and buy a house that ends up being a money pit. It happens. Take it as a learning experience.

- Don't let fear hold you back. Just get started.

- Just start and do it. Jump in headfirst.

LEARN PROPERTY MANAGEMENT

In my opinion, new landlords should self-manage their first property so that they understand the business and gain experience in every aspect. You may have a full-time job and feel like you couldn't handle managing your property on top of the job. Consider this: property management companies generally charge up to 10 percent. That means they take 10 percent off the top of the rent collected. That can add up quickly and eat into your profit.

Whether or not you hire a property manager might depend on your cash flow, how close you live to the property, and the type of property. I have two out-of-state vacation property rentals and both are being managed by someone else, but Rick and I manage the rest.

After Rick and I bought our first rental property, there were many times when we wondered if we did the right thing—especially when it came time to dealing with maintenance.

In one of our first homes, we discovered the bathroom floor was weak from water damage caused by a toilet that had apparently been leaking for quite some time. Thankfully, a friend in construction repaired it for us. I thought Rick was going to have a heart attack watching him cut a hole in the floor to fix the damage! We quickly learned that if you're going to buy and rent older properties, you need to learn the basics in repairs and maintenance, or have a list of contractors who can take care of the issues you can't fix.

About those contractors: It's crucial to put together a list of reliable, trustworthy property maintenance professionals. There are so many undependable workers in the area of repairs. This is another way your real estate agent can help. They will have a list of reliable, licensed professionals you can call.

If you're going to self-manage, look for a house within thirty minutes of where you currently live. You will get tired of driving back and forth to handle maintenance, preparation for new tenants, showing the property to potential tenants, and so on. This is why we eventually sold our first three rental properties and invested in the town where we currently live.

If you decide to hire a property management company, ask for referrals from your real estate agent and other people who have property management in place. Then interview several companies to make sure they're a good fit. For questions to ask potential companies and for information on the "good, bad, and the ugly" of property management in general, check out the video "Property Management: Should You Do It or Not?" on my Down Home Money YouTube channel (and be sure to subscribe for great weekly stories on passive income from ordinary people doing extraordinary things).

VET YOUR TENANTS

If you're handling property management, then you will be vetting potential tenants. This means running credit and background checks. We pay for a background check service so we don't have to deal with it ourselves. To find a screening service, google "tenant screening." You can probably get set up for as low as $19.95 per tenant screening. Some screening companies allow tenants to go online, fill in the information, and pay the fee, and then the company sends you the report. Do your research and pick the best company for you.

In thirty-one years of renting properties, we've had only six evictions. One way to cut down on problematic tenants is to set clear criteria up front. For example, you could require that applicants meet some or all of the following criteria:

- credit score minimum
- at current job for at least ____ years (you can decide how many)
- no previous evictions
- no smoking
- no pets (or limit the number or type of pets)

No matter what criteria you set, it's important to be fair, consistent, and honest with all of your tenants.

When you find yourself with good tenants, do what you can to keep them around. We have two amazing tenants in one of our duplexes. They wanted to hire their own landscaper to take care of the lawn and plants. We told them to go for it! You want tenants to take pride in your property because they will treat it like it belongs to them.

Rick and I now know how to turn around a rental quickly. We have a system for doing the walk-through. We explain to the tenants exactly what they need to do to get their security deposit back. We love being able to give back deposits because our turnaround time is decreased if we don't have to paint, replace the carpet, and so on.

RUN THIS LIKE A BUSINESS

Buying rental property is a business, and you have to treat it that way. If you treat it like a hobby, it will cost you money.

As you would for any business, keep a profit and loss statement for each of your rental properties. The profit-loss statement I use for my properties can be found on my website (downhomemoney.com) in the Money Tools section. It's a simple Excel spreadsheet that I fill out monthly so I can track income and expenses all year. After I fill in the numbers for December, the statement is ready to go to my accountant at tax time. As I've said, documentation beats conversation, and that's true with keeping track of your rental property business, too.

It might take you fifteen to thirty minutes a week to document any expenses you've had on your rental property. My process of documentation and keeping a profit-loss statement is very simple. I follow the KISS method: keep it simple, stupid. Why complicate it? We complicate money enough as it is. One of my goals with this book is to show you how simple it is to pursue financial freedom.

When I interviewed Randy, he told me he is always ready to conduct business, and he recommends others do the same. "I always have a contract in my truck," he said. "Me and my buddy were heading out to play basketball when we saw a For Sale by Owner sign, and I said, 'Well, buddy, hang on a bit.' I pulled off the side of the road, knocked on the door, and bought the property right there and wrote the contract." Now, that is being prepared!

TRY HOUSE HACKING

If I were in my twenties, I would go buy a duplex and house-hack my way to financial freedom.

House hacking is an investing strategy that involves renting out part of your primary residence to generate income to offset expenses such as mortgage, insurance, taxes, and even utilities. If you bought a duplex, you could live on one side and rent out the other and have someone else pay for your asset.

Additionally, if you move into one side of the duplex, you could qualify for an FHA (Federal Housing Administration) loan, which is only available if the home is your primary residence. A multiunit building (up to four units) counts if you live in one of the units. For example, you could buy a fourplex, move into one of the units, and rent the other three. The rent will more than cover your mortgage payment, so you're basically living there for free. You can take the money you're not using for your mortgage and use it to pay off debt, save for another rental, or invest in a retirement account.

With an FHA loan, you only have to put 3.5 percent down.

That means you could buy a $200,000 property with a $7,000 investment plus closing costs, and chances are good that the tenant(s) in the other unit(s) will cover most of your mortgage. You could also buy a single-family dwelling and rent out rooms to cover all or part of your mortgage, which is what Nick did (his story coming soon, promise!).

An FHA loan isn't necessarily for first-time home buyers, but that's often who takes advantage of this loan. With an FHA loan, you can have lower credit scores than you can with conventional loans.

If you're a veteran, you can qualify for a VA loan and pay no money down. Again, you could buy a multiunit building (up to four units), live in one unit, rent out the rest, and have your mortgage covered with money to spare.

I recently coached a guy at my office into his first rental property. He bought a duplex, and he's moving into one side with a roommate and renting out the other side. With rent from both, he will make $200 free and clear after paying his mortgage and utilities. He's putting that money straight into a Vanguard account to start his retirement.

If you can find one in your price range, a duplex is an excellent first rental property even if you don't live in it. If one tenant moves out, you still have income from the other side, which is crucial when you first start.

SACRIFICE NOW

I recently watched a documentary called *Playing with FIRE* about the FIRE (Financial Independence, Retire Early) movement. The film clearly shows the sacrifices and delayed gratification involved on the journey to financial independence. It also shows the end result: buying back time and having the freedom to create one's life by design, instead of being anxiety ridden and stressed out by trying to keep up with the Joneses.

The documentary follows Scott and Taylor Rieckens, a couple who lived in San Diego, California (Scott directed the film and also wrote a book with the same title). Scott and Taylor both had great jobs and made a lot of money, but they were also spending every penny they made. They ate at fine restaurants, lived in an expensive house, and owned luxury cars. Then they had a child and realized they had no time for their family because they were working long hours to support their consumerism. They were stuck.

They finally decided they wanted freedom more than a luxury car.

At one point, Taylor tells Scott what gives her joy: family time and being with their daughter. Neither of these things cost money. Too many people give their best at the office to make money to buy things, and then bring their tired selves home to the ones who really matter.

NICK'S STORY: PASSIVE INCOME AT TWENTY-EIGHT YEARS OLD

I don't come from a real estate background. My mom is a college professor and my dad is a human resources manager. Before I came along, the only house they ever owned was the one they lived in. When it came to investing, my parents were like most people and just stuck to the basic 401(k) and employer retirement plans.

My best friend's parents, however, were in the real estate business. My friend and I met in kindergarten, and although as a kid I had no idea what real estate was, I couldn't help but notice that the homes they moved into kept getting bigger and bigger. They started out in a one-story house, then moved to a three-story house, and finally moved into a four-story home *with* an elevator. (Did I mention it was on the lake and had a basketball court?) I decided that whatever my friend's parents did for work, I should probably do that, too.

That's when my entrance into this world really began. I started asking questions and learning. Growing up around my friend's parents, I learned about money, real estate, investing, and how to be wealthy—basically, all the important stuff that they don't teach you in school. They let me tag along to countless seminars, foreclosure auctions, and home renovations and taught me things that became the basis for much of what I do today. If you've ever read the book *Rich Dad Poor Dad*, it was kind of like my best friend's family was the rich dad teaching me what I needed to know about money.

Fast-forward a few years: I graduated from college and looked for my first real-world job. I obtained my real estate license when I was eighteen and worked on and off in my local real estate office while in college. However, during that time I had a terrible realization: I didn't actually like being a real estate agent. This led me down a dark path for a bit, what I call my quarter life crisis. I thought I had known all along my life plan, but it turned out, I had no idea at all. Eventually, I decided that I still loved real estate, but I needed to find my own path in this field.

Through some connections, I was able to get a great job after college with a custom home builder. Looking back, I realize how ironic it was to choose this job over being an agent because the entire sales process for designing and building a home from scratch was much longer and more difficult than just selling an existing home. But my experience working there proved invaluable as I learned a lot about the construction side of real estate and honed my skills in general sales and cold calling.

It was during this time that my thoughts turned back to investing. I loved the company I worked for but knew I didn't want to sell custom homes forever. I started listening to podcasts and reading books about investing, and over time I became convinced that this could really be my true path in real estate. I think the best way to figure out what you want to do in life is to first find out what you *don't* want to do.

I bought my first house in 2015 while still working for the custom home builder. I wasn't really thinking of being an investor; I just wanted to get out of my parents' house. Why rent when for just 5 percent down I could own something?

It was pretty easy to recruit some of my friends to live with me as they were also eager to get out of their parents' houses, and $400 a month was a steal for living in a decent four-bedroom house. It was also a steal for me since, after collecting their rent, I paid about $200 a month for my mortgage. Back then, I didn't even know what the term *house hacking* meant or that that's what I was doing; I just did it.

And that's how I ended up with my first three houses. We lived in one for about a year, I saved up money for another down payment, looked for another house, and then moved my roommates to the next place while I kept the previous house and rented it out. (Tip: Make sure you have flexible friends if you're going to try this strategy.)

That was about the time I began dreaming of being a full-time real estate investor and flipping and buying rentals on a more active basis. I knew that I was going to do it "one day" but never felt like I was ready for it. I always thought, *When I get to a certain point, I'll leave my job and do this for real.*

Then something happened that turned out to be the kick in the pants

I needed: the home building company I was working for went out of business. It had been a long, drawn-out process, but by the time the dust settled, we had gone from sixty employees to six—and somehow, I was one of them.

Our CEO decided to fold that company and start with a new fresh company. I remember him taking me out to pizza and describing the plans for the new company and inviting me to be a part of it. But the next day as I was walking around Home Depot picking out tile and backsplash for the first real flip I had recently purchased, I decided it was now or never. I called my CEO that very moment, thanked him for the opportunity to be a part of his new company, and told him I was out.

I made that phone call in 2017 and took the leap to become a full-time real estate investor. As of right now, I have flipped six houses and own five rental properties. I've managed $80,000 and even $150,000 remodels and made quite a few mistakes along the way. I've had many sleepless nights and plenty of dreams about my houses spontaneously falling apart. I've had fights with contractors and construction materials stolen from a property. But through it all, I've been blessed to be able to provide for myself and finally find my niche in real estate.

During a particularly difficult season, I walked into my property manager's office, and after telling him about all my problems, I threw out the question, "Why do I keep doing this?" He laughed a little and then replied, "Because you love it." And that's the truth.

You have to decide how committed you are to pursuing financial freedom and generating passive income. You may need to make some serious changes in your spending habits to bring down your monthly expenses so you can save your money for your future. If you live in an expensive place, you may have to move, both to reduce your rent or mortgage and to live closer to affordable rental properties. The couple in *Playing with FIRE* ultimately left San Diego because they could live somewhere else for a lot less money. Pursuing financial freedom sometimes requires tough choices and hard work, but it's so worth it in the long run.

IT'S NEVER TOO LATE TO START

My brother, Milt, lives in Kentucky and has worked for the same company for twenty years. He's in his late fifties, and until 2019, he had never invested in real estate besides his personal home. He was counting on his pension to fund his retirement.

Then Milt's company declared bankruptcy. This meant his retirement income will be greatly reduced when he does retire, so he looked for another way to provide income. After watching his little sister invest in real estate for many years, Milt finally decided to jump in and buy rental properties. When the student is ready, the teacher will show up!

By working with a local banker, Milt was able to get some creative financing, including no down payment on a couple of his purchases. This is another reason why having a great bank or lender relationship is so important.

Milt bought his first rental property at auction for $49,000. He got a conventional loan for $53,900 at 5.5 percent interest. His total monthly payment including taxes and insurance is $445 a month. He's renting it for $650, which means he's making $205 a month.

He then bought his second house for $35,000, but it appraised for $42,000. When banks write up loans, they look at the value-to-debt ratio. When a property appraises higher than the purchase price, it has built-in equity. In other words, the bank could get more than the original purchase price if the buyer defaulted on the loan.

As a result of the higher appraisal, the local bank gave Milt a loan with no money down, though he did have to pay $2,000 for closing costs and for the points to buy a lower interest rate. His mortgage, taxes, and insurance total $300 a month, and the house rents for $800—a gross profit of $500.

Toward the end of 2019, Milt bought a third house for $22,000. Again, the house appraised higher than the purchase price—$39,000 versus $22,000—so he had immediate equity and was able to get a loan with no money down and only $1,000 in closing costs. His mortgage with taxes and insurance total $250 a month, and he can rent it for $600, giving him a gross profit of $350.

As of this writing, Milt has a fourth house under contract. He offered $25,000, and he thinks he'll be able to rent it for $800 a month. When it's all official, he will likely have around $1,500 a month in passive income from these four properties.

As you can see, cheap houses are still out there, but you have to search for them. Milt doesn't wait for them to appear on Zillow or the MLS (Multiple Listing Service). Like Randy, he drives around neighborhoods looking for houses that are For Sale by Owner. If he sees a vacant house, Milt talks to the neighbors on either side to find out if they know who owns the vacant house. Remember, financial freedom takes work. You have to be willing to do what others aren't.

HEATHER'S STORY: JOURNEY TO FIRE

My husband, Brandon, and I graduated with our bachelor's degrees and then relocated to the Cincinnati area for his first big-boy job at one of the largest marketing research companies in the world. We planned to stay there for two to three years and then Brandon would go back for an MBA. I got a job downtown a few blocks from him, and we both began our corporate life. After the first year, we started making plans for the MBA. We would browse through the courses offered and were always drawn to the real estate classes. We planned that after an MBA, we would have the money and ability to start investing in real estate.

We rented an apartment for the first year. When we first moved in, we planned to stay there until the MBA. But when we were approaching our year mark, we started thinking about buying a house. It just made sense to do it. It seemed a little risky because we might have to sell in a couple of years, but we wanted to try homeownership. We bought a house that needed a little work and immediately started some fixer-upper projects. Brandon had some background in construction, so that helped us a lot.

We wanted to start a family and we struggled with infertility. We were excited to find out when we were finally expecting a baby boy! As we approached my due date, I was thinking more and more about what we would do for child care. At that point, I was working full time, forty hours a week at a corporate headquarters. I loved the people I worked with and it was a fantastic place for me for two years out of college, but I never felt like I would be able to meet my potential there.

After a lot of thought, we agreed that I would leave that job so I could be home with our son. We had the agreement, however, that I would have to come up with a way to support our family income. I already had six piano students and thought about scaling that business, but it didn't make sense because I would have to book my schedule out with several lessons every week. The point was that I wanted to be with our son and also needed to provide income.

When our son was only a few months old, we found a deal on a house a few doors down from our current home. We bought that house, sold our home as For Sale by Owner, and walked away from the sale with a $15,000 check. But when we moved into the next house, it needed work and this time we had a newborn. We struggled to fix it up and balance everything, but we knew there was something to real estate investing. We just weren't quite doing it right yet. Selling our first home gave us the first glimpse of our future.

The same month I left my job, we got our first official flip under contract. I bid on it through Auction.com and coordinated a hard money loan (a short-term loan with a higher interest rate) to fund it. It needed cosmetic work and we started work immediately after we closed. We had a few high school boys helping us do some work, but we primarily did the work ourselves. We finished the work in four weeks and were able to sell the house pretty quickly. While it was under contract to sell, we got our next purchase under contract via another hard money loan. It was one project to the next for us after that.

During that first flip, we had a big decision to make. Brandon was working sixty hours a week at his job and would then join me on the renovation projects in the evenings and weekends. We made the decision to commit 100 percent. Instead of giving away sixty hours a week of Brandon's time and efforts to another company, we chose to put those efforts toward building our own business. Brandon quit his corporate job. It was absolutely terrifying for us because we left everything "stable" including his salary income.

The next six months were probably the most difficult for us. The only thing that kept us going was our hope for a better life and the ability to change our future. There is a verse in the Bible that hit us hard. Haggai 1:5-7: "Ye have sown much, and bring in little...he that earneth wages earnest wages to put it into a bag with holes." We didn't want to keep working paycheck to paycheck our whole lives. If we could hang on tight for a few years and build up our passive income, we would be able to reach our goals.

Over the next six months, we rehabbed four more houses. After we sold the second house, we realized that we needed to start holding properties to build our wealth and passive income. We found creative finance strategies that allowed us to remodel the properties and partner with others to keep them. One of those houses we specifically bought with the vision to make it an Airbnb (short-term rental). We purchased that house for $14,000 and did a $50,000 rehab. When the work was done, it appraised at $116,000. It was our most dramatic project yet.

We had tons of doubts when we listed the house on Airbnb because there were so many other properties in our area, but the same night we activated the listing, we started getting reservations. Our first full month, we earned $3,800! A regular rental would have brought in $800 a month. Our monthly expenses were about $1,000, which meant we had an earned profit of $2,800. That was shocking to us! We had more monthly passive income from that one property than we did from my corporate job working forty hours a week. Obviously, we were motivated to repeat the process.

We have been working on our real estate career full time since August 2018, but it took us until December 2019 to feel like we were picking up momentum. We currently have two long-term rentals and two short-term rentals. I got my real estate license early in 2019. Brandon is still working on remodeling projects and flips.

We have obsessively been reading, listening, and learning about real estate the entire time. We listen to podcasts and videos, read books and articles, attend live classes, etc. We feel like our future is in our hands now and the possibilities are endless! We are still exhausted every day, and we keep going because we feel and see so much hope.

REMEMBER THE GOAL

Investing in real estate was the smartest financial decision I ever made. It truly made me a millionaire—or should I say, my tenants made me a millionaire. They paid for those properties month after month, and my net worth grew year after year as a result.

As Chris mentioned in his story, financial freedom through real estate investments allowed him to serve his community as an elected official. It gave Randy the option of not having to be anywhere at any certain time. He loves having the freedom to travel and goes to Vegas often with his friends. He also uses his financial freedom to give back to his parents and help them.

The people featured in this chapter are all ordinary people, just like you. They worked hard, earned their money, saved it, and took the extra steps necessary to break into real estate investment. And they are now enjoying a steady passive income stream as a result.

The next two chapters discuss other options for building passive income. We'll start with dividends and investments.

MYRA'S BEST PRACTICES FOR BUILDING A RENTAL PORTFOLIO

1. Start saving money to buy your rental property and build your reserve account.

2. Get prequalified with a bank or mortgage lender so you know what you qualify for before you start looking.

3. Select a real estate agent with a rental portfolio in the area you want to buy.

4. Decide your price point, your bottom line for monthly income from rent, and the area you want to search.

5. Have your agent set up search using your price and other criteria.

6. Do your due diligence related to inspections and knowing the rental market.

7. Get to know other landlords and compare notes.

8. If you decide to self-manage the property, develop a list of reliable contractors. If you decide to hire a property management company, find a reliable manager.

9. Run this like a business.

10. Jump in headfirst! Everything is fixable. You got this!

CHAPTER 6

Retirement and Brokerage Accounts

When I first started cutting hair in 1987, I would walk around the mall where the barbershop was located, trying to get new clients. Early on, I saw this one middle-aged gentleman who was clearly well-to-do. I walked right up to him and said, "Sir, my name's Myra and I cut hair. I can give you the best haircut you've ever had."

My Kentucky accent, big personality, and even bigger hair won him over. Five minutes later, Bob was sitting in my chair.

"You are quite the salesperson, young lady," he said. "You got me into your chair, and I don't even need a haircut. I just had it cut last week."

And with that, Bob became my client for the next twelve years.

One day as he sat in my chair, Bob asked me what I was doing for my retirement.

"I don't know," I replied. "I'm in my twenties!"

"You need to start now."

I just blew it off and didn't think much about it. I cut Bob's hair every four weeks, so every four weeks we continued our conversation about retirement and planning for the future. He kept telling me that because I was self-employed, I should open a SEP retirement account. He said it would be the smartest thing I ever did, but I still ignored his advice.

This conversation continued for years. Every four weeks, Bob pulled up in his shiny Lexus wearing the finest designer suits. When he sat in my chair, he flashed a gold diamond Rolex that could have blinded me. Finally I thought, *Maybe I should listen to Bob. He's obviously successful.*

So one day, I asked Bob what I should do.

"Open a SEP account with Vanguard," he said. "Buy shares of the Vanguard 500 Index Fund, and contribute to that account every month."

Bob went on to explain that an index fund is made up of

several stocks, so one stock may do well and balance out the one that does poorly.

"You'll be a millionaire one day if you do what I tell you," Bob said. "It will be sooner than you think."

Now he was speaking my language! I wanted to be a millionaire by the time I was thirty. That had always been one of my goals.

In April 1998, I finally took Bob's advice and opened a retirement account with Vanguard. I started contributing $100 a month, first by mailing a check and later through direct withdrawal from my checking account. Because I was focused on building a rental portfolio at the time, I didn't really pay attention to the balance of that account, but I consistently deposited money every month.

Well, my consistency paid off!

In December 2009, about eleven years after I opened that account, my balance reached $165,991.23. Over the next ten years, I continued making monthly investments. As my passive income from our rental properties increased, I contributed more to the account, but I didn't change anything about the investment portfolio itself. I just continued buying shares of the Vanguard 500 Index Admiral Fund (back then, its symbol was VFINX; today, it is VFIAX).

By the end of 2019, the balance of my account was—drum roll, please—over $1.1 million! In ten years, it had increased more than $970,000, and all I did was consistently make a monthly deposit. Compound interest did the rest! For something I didn't initially pay attention to or focus on as part of my financial freedom plan, my SEP has certainly given me a great return on investment.

In 2019, I read a book titled *The Simple Path to Wealth* by J. L. Collins. This book explained in simple terms how index fund investing provides passive income, and it prompted me to take a closer look at my portfolio. I decided to open a brokerage account with Vanguard and started buying shares of a different index fund—Vanguard Total Stock Market Index Fund (VTSAX). I had seen firsthand how index funds could create passive income, so I became more purposeful in creating wealth through dividends investment.

Dividends (or income returns) from investments are a simple way to fund your long-term financial freedom. With regular contributions, you can use the power of compound interest to create a passive income, both now and in retirement.

This chapter will give you an overview of your investment account options, along with resources for more information. I am not expert in investments, so I will point you to people who are. Although this income stream does require more money and longer period of time than investing in real estate, it also requires less work—no tenants calling about clogged toilets or broken water heaters. As many in the FIRE community have found, it's possible to live off the passive income from brokerage investments.

START WHERE YOU ARE AND LET IT RIDE

In chapter 4, we talked about evaluating your spending and cutting back where possible. Now I want to suggest that you take some of that money you've saved and invest in your future.

Let's say you spend $5 a day on a grande Frappuccino and you visit your favorite Starbucks five days a week. That's $25 a week or $100 a month. If you stopped visiting Starbucks twenty times a month and instead invested that $100 in a retirement account, you would earn compound interest on your money and take a big step toward financial freedom.

What is compound interest? It's the interest you receive on the initial balance, which includes all of the accumulated interest. In other words, it's interest on your interest. According to Grant Sabatier, creator of Millennial Money and author of my favorite book of 2019, *Financial Freedom: A Proven Path to All the Money You Will Ever Need*, "Compounding exponentially increases the value of your money over time, even if you don't increase your investments, because interest grows interest...The key to fast-tracking financial freedom is to speed up compounding by making and investing as much money as early and frequently as you can."[12]

Because of compounding, starting young and consistently investing small increments of money makes a big difference over time. If you can increase those regular deposits over time, even better!

Figure 6.1 illustrates what you would end up with at age sixty-five if you contribute $250 a month in an investment that earns 8 percent annually. As you can see, the difference between staring at age twenty-five and thirty-five is huge: over $500,000![13]

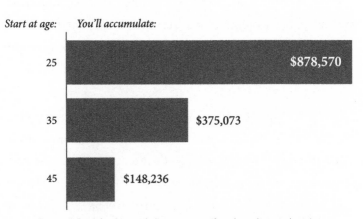

Start Early

Start at age: *You'll accumulate:*

25     $878,570

35     $375,073

45     $148,236

Figure 6.1. Don't let this graph discourage you if you haven't started yet. Let it motivate you to open an account and start contributing now!

Warren Buffett is considered one of the most successful investors in the world, and his advice regarding investing is simple: take your money, invest it, let it ride, and you'll be wealthy. Rather than put your money in a managed account where someone is making trades on your behalf, invest in an index fund or other assets and let it sit. This worked for me! I didn't chase the market or research new funds. I just contributed to the same fund every month and let it ride.

The same applies during economic downturns. Don't freak out and sell! When the market dropped after 9/11, during the 2008 financial crisis, and during the 2020 COVID pandemic, I just let it ride. History shows time is your friend, and over time, your money with grow and compound. Don't panic! Stay the course!

If you are scared of stocks, put your money in CDs, a money market account, or a savings account. Check Bankrate.com for the best interest rates so you can maximize your earning potential. You will earn less in a money market or savings account than you will in an investment account, but the risk is also lower. The important thing is to get started.

MYRA'S MOMENT

If you use a financial advisor, look for one who charges for their time or service, not commissions. You want someone who is paid by the hour or fee for services rendered because they will take time to look closely at your portfolio and give you sound advice.

If you're ready to take the plunge into stocks, the next two sections are for you. First, we'll discuss retirement accounts, which will provide income in your sixties and beyond. Then we'll discuss brokerage accounts, which can earn dividends toward your financial freedom now, though it will take time and money to get there.

Either way, I recommend using Vanguard.com as a resource. The website has articles and tools to help you figure out what kind of account is best for you.

RETIREMENT ACCOUNTS

In chapter 1, we discussed several reasons for planning your financial future: disappearing pensions, decreasing Social Security benefits, inflation, and longevity. It's important to start contributing now, even if it's only $100 a month to start with. By starting now, you can take advantage of compound interest and get the most out of your investments (remember the graph in figure 6.1).

THE 4 PERCENT RULE

How much do you need to have for retirement? Good question! Experts suggest using the 4 percent rule to figure out the answer.

The S&P 500 Index originally included 90 stocks. Then in

1957, it expanded to include 500. Studies show that average rate of return between 1957 and 2018 is roughly 8 percent.[14] Based on this number, financial advisors generally agree that 4 percent is a safe amount for retirees to withdraw as annual income while maintaining a steady account balance. If someone withdraws 4 percent, that leaves another 4 percent to cover inflation and allow for continued growth.[15]

Here's what the 4 percent rule looks like in real numbers. If your freedom number is $50,000 a year in retirement (approximately $4,100 a month), multiply that by twenty-five years to figure out how much you would need total to withdraw 4 percent a year and still have enough:

$50,000 (annual withdrawal) × 25 (years in retirement) = $1.25 million

In other words, you would need to have a portfolio of $1.25 million dollars to throw off 4 percent annually for twenty-five years.

If you need $100,000 a year to maintain your current lifestyle, then your equation would look like this:

$100,000 (annual withdrawal) × 25 (years in retirement) = $2.5 million

In other words, you would need to have a portfolio of $2.5

million dollars to throw off 4 percent annually for twenty-five years.

This lump sum is what we call your financial independence (FI) number—total amount saved to give off monthly or yearly income so that you will not have to trade time for work.

It may take up to twenty years to build up a retirement account with $1.25 million dollars. This is why it is important to start contributing now so it has time to grow and compound. This is also why it's important to develop multiple passive income streams—including rental properties (chapter 5) and side hustles or small businesses (chapter 7)—to make sure you have enough to live comfortably in retirement.

It's easy to get overwhelmed and become paralyzed and not do anything. Don't do it! Stay focused on the goal and get started. For me, buying rental properties was a faster path, so that's what I chose as the way to build passive income. The key is to take action. I diligently contributed to my retirement account, and look what happened.

TYPES OF ACCOUNTS

Disclaimer: I am not a financial expert. That's part of the reason I wanted to write this book—to show that you don't have to be a financial expert to achieve financial freedom. You simply have to set up and be consistent in your saving habits. It truly is not how much you make but how much you keep and what you do with it!

My suggestion is to contact an expert. Vanguard is my favorite investment firm because the fees are low, and the website has great tutorials and a list of questions to walk you through your decision regarding a retirement account. Answer the questions, and Vanguard will tell you which account to open. It's that simple.

You get to choose when you want to take withdrawals from your retirement account, as early as fifty-nine and a half. Generally, you must take your first required minimum distribution (RMD) by April 1 of the calendar year following the year you turn seventy-two (prior to 2020, it was age seventy and a half). For each subsequent year, you have to take your annual RMD by December 31. If you withdraw less than the minimum, you may owe a 50 percent penalty tax on the difference. Once you start taking withdrawals, you'll be paying taxes on that income. The only exception is a Roth IRA. The money in a Roth has already been taxed.

Here's a brief summary of the different types of individual retirement accounts (IRAs). The type you choose will depend on your financial situation and income.

Roth IRA

A Roth offers tax-free growth and tax-free withdrawal in retirement—tax-free because the money contributed has already been taxed. As long as you own your Roth for five years before you start making withdrawals and as long as you wait until you're fifty-nine and a half before you start making withdrawals, you will not owe federal taxes on the money you draw during retirement. With a Roth IRA, there is no RMD as long as you are alive.

You can set up a Roth independent of any retirement account set up through your employer. Because this account is yours, separate from your place of employment, there are no employer-plan restrictions. You can set up and contribute to a Roth in addition to any employer retirement plan (such as a 401(k) or 403(b)) as long as you don't earn more than the IRS income limit for Roth plans. In 2020, the adjusted gross income limit for a single person is up to $139,000, and for a married couple filing jointly, it's $206,000.

There is also a limit on how much you can contribute annually to a Roth. In 2020, the cap on the annual contribution to a Roth is $6,000 for people under fifty years old and $7,000 for people fifty or older.

Traditional IRA

If you open a traditional IRA, your contributions will come

from pretax money. This means two things: (1) you can write off your contributions on your taxes each year, and (2) you will be taxed when you start making withdrawals.

Unlike a Roth, there is no income limit with a traditional IRA. Like a Roth, the traditional IRA has an annual contributions limit: $6,000 for individuals under fifty and $7,000 for individuals fifty and older.

You must take your first RMD from your traditional IRA by April 1 of the year following the year you reach age seventy-two (age seventy and a half before 2020).

SEP IRA

A SEP (simplified employee pension) is for anyone who is self-employed, owns a business, employs other people, or earns freelance income. Like a traditional IRA, the money contributed to a SEP has not been taxed, which means you can write off your contributions each year. It also means you will be taxed when you started making withdrawals.

In 2020, the cap on the annual contribution to a SEP is 25 percent of the employee's total compensation, up to $57,000, whichever is less. If you're self-employed, your contributions are limited to 20 percent of your net income (figured from the net profit determined on IRS schedule C minus the deductible self-employment tax).

BROKERAGE ACCOUNTS

In 2010, Grant Sabatier was twenty-four years old and living in his parents' basement. One day, he wanted a burrito for lunch, but he had only $2.26 in his bank account. That was a wake-up call. Five years later, Grant had a net worth of over $1.25 million, and by age thirty, he had reached financial freedom. How did he do it? Read his book to find out! In *Financial Freedom: A Proven Path to All the Money You Will Ever Need*, Grant takes the reader on his journey to passive income through portfolio investment in index funds.

As part of his strategy, Grant opened a brokerage account to do his index fund investing. With a brokerage account, you deposit money like you would in a bank, but then you use that money to buy and sell stocks and invest in index funds, exchange traded funds, and more. When your investments increase in value, you earn dividends, which you can reinvest or receive as income.

Each investment firm has a different minimum deposit for opening a brokerage account. It's completely up to you how that money is invested, so you'll need to do some research if you pursue this option. In theory, you could invest in the same funds as you do in your retirement account. The difference is that with a brokerage account, you have the option of receiving dividends now as income, whereas your retirement account dividends will continue growing until you reach retirement age and start making withdrawals as income.

As mentioned in chapter 5, it takes a lot of money to earn a sufficient income stream from a dividend investment portfolio income stream—possibly hundreds of thousands of dollars. My suggestion is to start building your passive income stream through a rental portfolio because you can break in with a smaller up-front investment. At the same time, start saving. When you have more money to invest, open a brokerage account to start working on your dividends passive income.

I also recommend maxing out your retirement account before you start playing with a brokerage account. Money going into your retirement account grows tax-free, whereas dividends received from a brokerage account will be taxed.

There are multiple paths to financial freedom. Whichever path you choose, a retirement account should be part of your strategy. It's important to pay yourself first, even if you start with $100 a month like I did.

In the next chapter, we'll discuss ways to earn more money through side hustles and small businesses. This income can be used to help you pay down debt, or it can be saved to invest in passive income streams such as real estate investment, retirement investment, or opening a brokerage account. Side hustles and small businesses can also turn into passive income streams themselves.

DO YOUR RESEARCH

Before you start investing through a brokerage account, I recommend doing some research. If you want to move forward in dividend investments, become a student of money.

Here's a list of books to start with:

- *Financial Freedom: A Proven Path to All the Money You Will Ever Need* by Grant Sabatier—Grant's journey to financial freedom through dividend investments

- *The Simple Path to Wealth: Your Road Map to Financial Independence and a Rich, Free Life* by J. L. Collins—written to help his daughter start investing

- *The Little Book of Common Sense Investing: The Only Way to Guarantee Your Fair Share of Stock Market Returns* by John Bogel—written by the founder of Vanguard to share his investing strategies

- *Your Money or Your Life: 9 Steps to Transforming Your Relationship with Money and Achieving Financial Independence* by Vicki Robin—groundbreaking book on seeing the real value of money

CHAPTER 7

Side Hustles and Small Businesses

I always knew I was going to be a business owner. As a child, I did side hustles before they were called side hustles. If there was money to be made, I was making it, whether it was babysitting, charging interest on money I loaned my mom and siblings, selling eggs from the hundred chickens my dad bought me, making button covers when that was a craze, or working two restaurant jobs in high school.

When I moved to Texas, I went to barber's school and knew that eventually I would own my own salon. One day, I was reading *The Dallas Morning News* classifieds, and there it was: Northtown Mall barbershop for sale. This was my opportunity to be a business owner.

The owner wanted to retire, but he still had three or four

years on his lease. He was selling the business and all of the equipment for $4,000, and he wanted someone to take over his lease, which was over $1,000 a month. Using my negotiating skills, I got him to finance the sales price interest free. On October 14, 1986, at the age of twenty, I gave the owner a down payment toward the $4,000 purchase price and officially became a business owner. Because I was frugal and didn't like being in debt, I saved enough to pay the balance in less than four months.

I worked long hours to get my new business off the ground, and it worked. When I opened my salon, I had zero customers. Within a year, I was booked out eight weeks in advance.

When it came time to negotiate my lease with the big commercial real estate company, I walked into that meeting of gray-haired men, naive as all get out, and fooled them into thinking I knew what I was talking about. I quickly learned to put on my big-girl panties and take charge. I took risks—sometimes they worked out and sometimes they didn't. This is how I learned. Failing forward is just part of being in business for yourself.

In August 1986, I met Rick Oliver, my future husband. Rick worked for the police department, with all of its danger and politics. He was intrigued by this twenty-year-old who was her own boss and made her own decisions, and he wanted the same kind of freedom.

So, in the midst of supporting and encouraging my long hours at the hair salon, Rick caught the business ownership fever and started his own side hustle buying and selling cars. He got his dealer's license and started buying cars at the Dallas Car Auction. He would fix them up and sell them out of the newspaper for profit. (Back then, the newspaper was very popular for finding good deals!) Then he bought a magnetic sign business and started a second side hustle making magnetic signs for people's cars.

For several years, we worked long hours at our small businesses and side hustles to create additional income, which we saved and invested in real estate to create passive income. Later on, I started a second business, which turned into a steady passive income stream itself (more on that later). To save money for reserves and investing, you may need to do the same. You may need to start a side hustle and work long hours to create another income stream. Are you willing to do that?

In this chapter, we'll talk about building businesses or side hustles to earn extra money and eventually to create another passive income stream. We'll discuss the pros and cons of three options—side hustles, small businesses, and franchises—and I'll share how I used all three paths to achieve financial freedom.

SIDE HUSTLES

A side hustle is just like it sounds: something you're doing on the side, in addition to your full-time job, to make more money.

TIPS, PROS, AND CONS

If you're in debt with limited savings, side hustles are probably the best place to start. The great news is that you can turn almost anything into a side hustle.

In Your Passion

My number one tip regarding side hustles is to make sure it's something you're passionate about, something you don't mind doing on nights and weekends in addition to your full-time job. You're going to be spending most of your free time on this side hustle, so make sure it's something you enjoy. Otherwise, you're going to burn out.

The options are endless when it comes to side hustles. Do you love dogs? Start a dog walking or dog sitting business. Do you mind ironing clothes? Start an ironing business. You saw what it did for the woman who paid cash for one of our rentals. Are you skilled in technology or graphic design? Offer your services on Fiverr to make extra money. Do you like browsing garage or estate sales? Repurpose and resell the stuff you find. Because of the internet, it's never been easier to make extra cash. You just have to decide what you're willing to do and go for it. Remember what my mama said: where there's a will, there's a way.

The question is, what are you willing to give up in order to move up? Working a successful side hustle will take time and energy, but anyone can do it. You don't have to be a financial expert; you simply have to be disciplined and be okay with delayed gratification.

Think back to chapter 3 and the questions about what gives you joy. Is there something in that list that you can turn into a side hustle? The sky is truly the limit in terms of what you can do. Here's a list of possible side hustles to get your creative juices flowing:

- Network marketing (e.g., Avon, Amway, Pampered Chef, Mary Kay, Nu Skin)
- Internet business selling artistic creations (e.g., Etsy shop or eBay store)
- Freelance writer, graphic designer, editor, spreadsheet creator (you could create a profile on Fiverr, Upwork, and other gig sites)
- Dog walking/grooming, pet sitting
- Driving for Uber or Lyft
- House cleaning, lawn mowing, landscaping
- Part-time job in your passion (e.g., coffee shop, bakery, consignment shop, outdoor retailer, running store, home

improvement, bartending, garage sale or flea market/flipper)
- Content creator for YouTube, Instagram, or Facebook
- Amazon affiliate/seller

Run It like a Business

My number two tip regarding a side hustle: run it like a business if you want it to pay you like a business. Part-time work is part-time money.

Part of running a side hustle like a business is creating a profit-loss statement, which tells you how much you spent and how much you earned. For example, if you take photographs and make note cards and then sell them, you would need to keep track of how much you spend on card stock, printing, and so forth, as well as what you make on each card sold.

Evaluate your profit-loss statement regularly to make sure you are earning a decent profit. Figure out how much time you spend making each thing you sell, as well as how much money you spend on the parts and pieces. If you spend two hours on each item and you have $18 invested in materials, you don't want to sell your creations for $20 each. You'd only be making $2, which is hardly worth your time. Do research to find out a reasonable price.

JAMIE'S STORY: FREEDOM THROUGH NETWORK MARKETING

I began network marketing in the late 1990s because of a weight-loss product that I was using in my nutrition practice. I was a full-time professor and pregnant with my first child, but I quickly saw the benefit of leveraged income. I had huge success with that company, even winning several trips and a new car. However, after a few years, the main product I used in my practice was changed, so I decided to switch companies. I always believed in network marketing and tried two other businesses before finding my home with my current company, Nu Skin Enterprise.

I have been a part of Nu Skin since 2006, and after two years part time, I was able to leave my job as a full-time nutrition professor and begin working from home. At that time, my children were in preschool, and working full time from home allowed me to be with them daily. I built my team and business from the ground up, around my family's schedule. Over the years, I have attended every school event, participated as Homeroom Mom for my children each school year, and volunteered on all field trips my children have attended! Most importantly, network marketing has given me not only financial freedom but time freedom as well!

This became evident in 2015 when both of my parents broke their backs within a week of each other. Due to the fact that I am an only child, both of their treatment and rehabilitation programs were highly dependent on my participation. If I had been working a traditional job, a boss would not have let me miss work as much as I did. In the fall of 2015, my father passed away, and because of network marketing, for the next few years I was able to take care of my mother until her passing in the summer of 2019. I can look back without any regrets because I had the opportunity of network marketing.

Also in 2015, my sixteen-year-old daughter joined me in Nu Skin. She built a tremendous team part time in high school and has continued to grow her business while in college. Her side hustle may turn into a full-time job after completing her degree. During the global COVID-19 pandemic, we both had our best months in the industry. We have been able to help others realize that some of their strengths may lie outside their current occupation.

My network marketing journey began as a side hustle for a favorite product, but it has become a full-time passion for a leveraged-income, nontraditional business opportunity. It has given my family a newfound freedom in ways, both financially and emotionally, that I could have never possibly imagined over twenty years ago.

In addition, make sure you know your numbers. Know how much is going in, how much is going out, and what your profit is. It's that simple. A balance sheet has your business's assets and liabilities. As with your personal net worth sheet (see chapter 4), your business's balance sheet has equipment, bank accounts balances, inventory, and prepaids in the assets column and expenses, debt, or funds owed in the liabilities column.

In chapter 5, you read Nick's story about real estate investment. In addition to his investment passive income, Nick built a side hustle that costs him zero money. He spends two hours a day on the telephone calling new real estate licensees to tell them about Keller Williams Realty's value proposition. If any of them come to Keller Williams and list Nick as their sponsor, he earns profit share. In 2019 alone, Nick made $10,000 in profit share simply by spending ten hours a week on the phone.

I once tried to make an appointment with Nick during his

lead-generation time slot, and he said he couldn't do it at that time because he was already booked. He treats that side hustle like a business, and his consistency has paid off, no doubt!

Here's a list of pros and cons related to side hustles:

PROS	CONS
1. You have autonomy. Nobody cares if you build the business or how you run it. It's your gig.	1. Because it's your gig, you don't have accountability. You have to be a self-motivator who can work even when no one is watching.
2. For the most part, side hustles are relatively low cost to start.	2. It may be stressful when you first launch. If you're already stretched thin financially, even the relatively low start-up cost may be tough until you start making money.
3. You get to work in your passion.	3. It could be a serious energy zapper that stretches you thin. That's why it's so important to get a side hustle in your passion.
4. You get to set your own schedule.	4. To turn a decent profit, you will most likely use all of your free time to work your side hustle. That means less time for hobbies, family, friends, vacations, and so on.

MY SIDE HUSTLE: NETWORK MARKETING

In 1996, while I was cutting hair, I built a network marketing business as a side hustle (this is where I met Jamie, whose story you read earlier). A nutritional supplement company sold a weight-loss product called Natural Trim that absolutely worked, so I started sharing it in my salon. Soon, I had sold enough to win a trip to Hawaii. About six months later, someone called to tell me I was one of the top five salespeople in the country.

"Congrats!" he said. "I'd love to come to Texas to show you how to build a passive income from this business." Now, this guy was speaking my language! Rick and I were already building a passive income stream with our rental portfolio, and this could be a way to earn more money to invest in more rental properties.

I packed out the hair salon to listen to this guy's presentation. He was an average Joe, nothing special except that he was making $30,000 a month selling Natural Trim and another product called Fat Free. I listened to his talk, mesmerized, because I knew if this guy could make $30,000 a month, then I could be a superstar—especially after I watched him spell millionaire with three *l*s! Within two years, I was the top distributor for the state of Texas.

In network marketing, you make more money when you sign people up on your team. You earn money from their sales as well as your own. Before the guy came to speak, I was making about $5,000 a month from selling the product alone. After that presentation, I started making an additional $3,000 to $8,000 a month, depending on how much my team sold.

I worked this network marketing side hustle from 1996 to 2002. Rick and I used the money earned to buy more rentals and to pay off the dream home we had purchased in 1998. In 1999, I sold my hair salon and retired, although I never really liked that word. I prefer saying I became financially free. We were living the dream, living off the passive income provided by our rental properties and my network marketing business. We had arrived!

SMALL BUSINESS OWNERSHIP

Another option for earning extra cash is small business ownership. As with side hustles, there are many options, depending on your interests, talents, and start-up funds. Here is a short list of ideas:

- Trades/talents: plumbing, electrical, landscaping, hair-styling, massage therapy, tattoo artist
- Services: real estate, food service (restaurant, coffee shop, bakery)
- Retail: used book store, consignment shop, specialty store

In general, small businesses require more up-front money than side hustles, so this isn't the place to start if you're in debt and have limited savings.

You can start your own business in any of these areas, or buy an existing one like I did when I bought the retiring barber's shop in the mall. Either way, small business ownership requires long hours and hard work. You're the boss, which means you have to make decisions, hire employees, fire employees, set prices, order supplies, pay bills, and so much more.

When I bought the barbershop, I had no clients. I started by walking around the mall giving away free haircuts to get people to try me. I put flyers on cars in the mall parking lot. I got to know all of the other business owners. Looking back, I think people were impressed by a twenty-year-old with great work ethic, and they wanted to help me out. Most kids my age were partying and having fun, and I was working my butt off. Cutting hair is my God-given talent, and I quickly built my clientele because people loved how I did their hair.

Your talent may not be cutting hair, but it might be as a tattoo artist or landscaper. How can you turn that into a business? It won't be easy, but if you have the drive, you can make it happen.

TIPS, PROS, AND CONS

When you start your business, don't be afraid to ask for referrals. Whenever a client would say, "Oh my gosh, I love my hair! This is the best it's ever looked," I would say, "Oh, I'm so happy for you! Would you please share that with a couple of your friends to help me build my business? I can keep my prices low if I can build a big business." People always responded positively. I received enough business that I kept my prices at $5 a haircut and $25 a perm for years, even though I could have tripled the price. I wanted to give value and have customers for life.

Another tip: Be the person who is dependable and consistent. Answer email and respond to phone calls. You never know how you touch people by doing so.

Here are some pros and cons of small business ownership as you consider whether this path is right for you:

PROS	CONS
1. With employees you have trained, you have leverage. You can duplicate your efforts and increase your income.	1. Your employees may not show up to work. Then what? If you own a restaurant, you might be flipping hamburgers or taking orders.
2. You have freedom and autonomy because you're your own boss. You set the hours, prices, and so on.	2. Business ownership can be stressful and time consuming. There's no written plan other than what you come up with, so you have to figure it out quickly and make it work.
3. A business has equity, or monetary value, so you could sell the business and the property that goes with it, just like the retiring barber sold me his shop and I later sold my salon to another stylist.	3. You are monetarily invested, so there is financial risk if the business doesn't do well.
4. You have opportunity for growth in so many areas, personally and professionally. You can grow your skills, mindset, competency in business, customer base, and more.	4. You have to be the jack-of-all-trades. When you're just starting out, you may not be able to hire a bookkeeper, for example, so you have to do it yourself.
5. There are no limitations except what you put on yourself. You have the freedom to make your business exactly what you want.	5. There's no security. There's no fallback. Small business ownership is do or die.

MY SMALL BUSINESS: REAL ESTATE

By 2001, I was getting bored of retirement. The network marketing company had undergone some changes, and it looked like my income would be dropping significantly (which it did starting in 2002). We continued building our rental portfolio, which was bringing in good money, but I had been wanting to build something like I had with the network marketing business, so I decided to get my real estate license.

I didn't really want to show houses, so I took a different path in real estate. In 2002, I started an apartment locating company and started renting properties. Apartment locating is when someone is offering their place to rent and they're willing to pay a real estate agent to rent it for them. The agent usually gets 50 percent of one month's rent as a fee, but sometimes I was paid a full month's rent. I represented the tenant in the transaction. I showed properties and negotiated the lease and sometimes got the tenants a deal, like a free month. I knew how to do that because I had been renting our own properties for a decade.

The first year, I rented over two hundred units and earned over $100,000. Making more money meant we could buy more rental properties and enjoy more fun-in-the-sun trips and other things we hadn't bought over the years because we had been saving and living frugally. I was motivated to keep working!

That first year when I focused on renting, I didn't sell one home. During my second year, some renters began calling me and saying, "Hey, you worked so hard to rent me something. Will you sell me a house?" Even though this wasn't my initial plan, I would have been a fool to say no. So I put together a database with all my tenants, I sent out marketing material, and I started selling houses like crazy. I officially got back on the treadmill of working for money because I'm very competitive and I love to win.

According to the National Association of REALTORS, eight out of ten agents don't make it and get out of the business in their first two years. That's a shame because if you put in the time, having your real estate license opens the door to building an incredible business with no limits on income. By 2006, I was back to working twelve hours a day selling real estate, but I was making over $200,000 a year.

In terms of small businesses, real estate is a huge opportunity to make lots of money and secure financial freedom with very little debt—if you're willing to hustle. It's not like paying thousands for a degree and then hoping you will get a job. There are no limits on how much money you can make as a real estate agent. You get to decide what you are worth!

FRANCHISES

In simple terms, a franchise is a license that allows the owner to provide a service or sell a product under the business's name. There are franchises in many different industries: food service/restaurants, plumbing, real estate, hair salon, car repair, and more.

TIPS, PROS, AND CONS

Franchises are something to keep in mind for your future self. This option can generate a solid income stream, but it also can involve a big up-front cost. It is much cheaper to start a side hustle or even a small business.

I built my own hair salon, and along the way I could have decided to turn it into a franchise. Hair salon franchises often approach independent hairstylists who have built successful salons and offer to buy them out. It happens with real estate companies and other small businesses as well.

Franchises are a great model because they have proven systems and model to follow on the road to success. At the same time, you have to be careful about which franchise you buy. Because of the time involved in some franchises, you might be buying a job instead of investing in a passive income stream.

Here's a short list of pros and cons to keep in mind:

PROS	CONS
1. Franchises come with a set of proven systems and tools. You simply follow the business plan the way it's laid out.	1. You can't run a franchise any way you want. You have to run it by corporate's systems, tools, policies, and guidelines.
2. Franchises have name recognition. The corporate office does a lot of the marketing and advertising for you. The brand is recognized across the country.	2. Owning a franchise is expensive. The up-front cost generally ranges from several hundred thousand to a million dollars. There are also ongoing franchise fees on each sale.
3. You receive hands-on training and support, with the opportunity to ask questions and have someone walk you through problem solving and troubleshooting.	3. Owning a franchise comes with a contractual agreement. If you don't run the business exactly according to the guidelines, you could lose your franchise.

MY FRANCHISE OPPORTUNITY: KELLER WILLIAMS

My journey to owning a franchise started with selling real estate, and then I became the Team Leader of a real estate office. When I proved I could double the business, I earned the right to have ownership inside a franchise. It took me thirteen years to go from selling real estate to owning a franchise, but it was well worth the effort. Here's how it went.

I had been selling real estate since 2001 and proved to be a natural-born salesperson. In December 2010, I was the President of the Greater Denton Wise County Association of REALTORS. I had accomplished everything I wanted in real estate, and I was ready to start having fun. We were making over $20,000 a month in passive rental income, and we were living debt-free. I was ready to slow down and enjoy the fruits of our labor.

Then I got the offer to run a Keller Williams office for $60,000 a year. Why would I leave my life of freedom to run an office and have a nine-to-five job making far less money? Because I love a challenge! I wanted to be a leader and help others see their potential. Plus, the owner of Keller Williams told me, "You go double my business and I will make you a partner." That meant one day I would earn passive income as a franchise owner. I worked hard for three years to make that happen and to own 30 percent of that office. It brings in an annual six-figure passive income stream. I have since bought into two other offices—one in Florence, Kentucky, and the other one in Columbus, Ohio. I am the Operating Principal for all three offices.

I had to go backward for a short time to move forward, but look where it got me today. As a franchise owner, I continue to make passive income through the three offices even though I no longer put up signs and sell houses. I have great leadership teams running these offices for me. My income is now considered passive.

There are so many opportunities to earn extra money to fund your financial freedom. As my story shows, side hustles and small businesses can lead to solid passive income streams and help you achieve financial freedom. The question is, how badly do you want financial freedom? If you're willing to put in the work to earn money to pay down debt, save, and invest in passive income streams, you can do it!

It's so easy to let fear paralyze you into not taking action. Your mind is a powerful thing, but you can control it! Yes, there are risks to side hustles and business ownership, but there are worse things to fear, like being broke at sixty years old and having to work until you're eighty. Take action now!

Being twenty, thirty, or forty years old with financial problems is fixable. You simply need to decide how. Are you going to stop spending money, get a better job, find a side hustle, or all of the above? Get focused on what you want out of life and make a plan to get there.

When you decide to jump in, email me at downhomemoney@gmail.com. I'd love to hear your success stories or consult with you on your next big thing.

Conclusion

BRINGING IT ALL TOGETHER

Congratulations! By finishing this book, you have taken a big step toward financial freedom. As promised, I kept it simple. Now I'm going to wrap it up for you and put a bow on it. You just have to open the package.

Where you are today is the result of your spending habits of the last five years, and where you will be in the future is the result of the decisions you make from this point on. Taking responsibility for your current financial situation is the first step to recovering and making a change. If you are aware of the problem, you can find a solution and work toward financial freedom. It all starts with shifting your mindset from scarcity to abundance. To reach financial freedom, you need to think big!

I'm living proof that the following plan works. Remember, I started this journey as a twenty-year-old hairstylist who got herself into debt and worked and saved her way out. I didn't start with loads of cash. I earned my money and learned to be purposeful with it. If you're willing to make some sacrifices, you can do the same.

YOUR FREEDOM PLAN

The following action plan summarizes lessons from this book and includes a few bonus tips for living your best life. Jump in today!

1. KNOW YOUR BIG WHY

To make sacrifices, change your spending habits, and save for you future, you must know your big why. You have to know what you're striving for.

Do you want the freedom to choose whether or not you work? Do you want the freedom to travel? Do you want to spend quality time with family and friends instead of giving them your tired, exhausted, overworked self? Those are reasons to be free. (If you're still not sure what your big why is, go back to chapter 3 and review the three questionnaires.)

If you don't have big goals and a big reason to be financially free, the plan I'm offering will not work. It's simple, but it's not easy. To pursue financial freedom, you have to sacrifice today and delay gratification. That process takes years. To stay on track, you will need to remind yourself daily why you are doing this.

2. DO YOUR NET WORTH SHEET

You have to know where you *are* to know where you *are going*. This is where your net worth sheet comes in. Remember, documentation beats conversation every time. So sit down and document your assets and liabilities. As we discussed in chapter 4, assets are anything you own that has real value (like your home), plus your retirement accounts and bank accounts. Liabilities include any money you owe on those items or other debts (for example, school loans or credit cards). Assets minus liabilities equals net worth.

If your liabilities are greater than your assets, your journey to financial freedom should start by earning more money (chapter 7) and paying down debt.

3. PAY DOWN DEBT

Paying down debt is a crucial part of achieving financial freedom. Debt is a monster that steals joy and freedom. It can take away your choice to work or not. If you are deep in debt, you may not be able to quit the job you hate because you have to pay the monster.

Don't be a slave to debt. Instead, take action! Make a list of the balance and interest rate on each credit card. Focus on the card with the highest interest rate and start paying down the balance. When that one is paid off, move on to the next. You have to make a conscious effort to pay down debt and purposely live on less. It should be a top priority.

4. LIVE ON A BUDGET

Okay, I've said it. You need to live on a budget. Do you make $3,000 a month? You cannot spend $4,000. You will never get ahead. In fact, in a few years you'll be so far in the hole you might never get out.

In 1946, Merle Travis, a coal miner from Muhlenberg County, Kentucky, wrote a song titled "Sixteen Tons."[16] In 1955, Tennessee Ernie Ford made it a hit. My daddy loved this song and used to sing it to me all the time. Some of the lyrics have stuck with me all these years later, and these words are perfect for us today:

You load sixteen tons, what do you get?

Another day older and deeper in debt

Saint Peter, don't you call me 'cause I can't go

I owe my soul to the company store

If you don't learn to live off a budget, you will owe your soul to consumer debt and you will be stuck in a job as a result. Learn to take control of your money instead of letting your money control you. It is very freeing.

Housing, food, insurance, and transportation will be the biggest expenses in your budget. You can use your documentation from chapter 4 to figure out how much to budget for other monthly expenses. Don't forget to include retirement contributions and saving for your passive income investments.

Regarding your housing budget, ask yourself this: are you living in more house than you need? A good rule of thumb is spending no more than one-third of your income on housing. If you're spending more, it might be time to downsize to save money for your future self.

It also might be time to sell your expensive car and buy something you can afford. Remember, a car is not an asset. It continues to decrease in value the longer you own it. Sell the car, buy one you can pay cash for, and put the money you save on monthly payments toward assets that give you a passive income. A car simply gets you from point A to point B, and when it's paid for, it drives like a luxury vehicle without a doubt.

Creating and sticking to a budget will come with tough choices. That's why you need to know your big why. Your purpose will give you a reason to not spend on things that won't matter tomorrow. Remember, you are building a financial empire so you have the freedom to choose what you want to do, rather than being stuck doing what you have to do. This results in a big difference in quality of life.

5. BUILD A RESERVE ACCOUNT

When you are writing out your budget, you should also include a line item for building a reserve money market account (a money market account earns more interest than a regular savings account). Your first savings goal should be one month's worth of expenses. Then save two months' worth. Your ultimate goal is to have six months' worth of reserves.

A reserve account provides a safety net for you and your family in case someone loses a job or you have a family emergency. Even if it's only $20 a month right now, start building your reserves account. I recommend having an automatic transfer into this account so it is a non-negotiable part of your budget.

A 2018 Federal Reserve report found that four in ten adults would not be able to cover an unexpected $400 expense. If you learn nothing else from this book, learn this: create a reserve savings account and work toward having a balance equal to six months of expenses. That will give you peace of mind knowing you are covered in case of an emergency.

6. TRACK EVERY PENNY

As discussed in chapter 4, most people hate this tip, but it's the most effective way to save money. Tracking every penny is how I learned what I was wasting my money on.

We have become accustomed to spending money and not evaluating what it actually costs to buy something. Do you know how much you are paid hourly? If you earn $40,000 a year, then you're making approximately $20 an hour. How often do you go out to eat and pay $20 for a meal? That means you worked an hour to pay for that food. If you know this up front, you may decide you don't need to eat out so often.

Tracking every penny helps you put things in perspective. When I started looking at how much I had to work to pay for a new pair of shoes, I realized quickly that I didn't need another pair of black sandals. The ones in my closet were just fine.

7. DECLUTTER YOUR HOME, DECLUTTER YOUR LIFE

When you declutter your home, you gain a different kind of freedom—freedom from stuff. We all have so many things we just don't need. I couldn't believe how much clarity and freedom I gained when I cleared out my closets and drawers. Now I do it once a year. A helpful book on this topic is *The More of Less* by Joshua Becker.

Another benefit of decluttering your home is that you can

sell the stuff you're getting rid of. You won't believe how much money you can make! Use that money to start or add to your reserve account, or start a retirement account and buy some index funds. If you've met your reserve account goal and you're contributing regularly to your retirement account, then go treat yourself to an ice cream! You are well on your way to financial freedom.

8. MAX OUT YOUR RETIREMENT CONTRIBUTIONS

Whether you have a traditional IRA, a Roth IRA, a SEP IRA, or a 401(k) through your employer, max that thing out. If your employer matches your contributions, even more reason to contribute the maximum allowable. (For a refresher on each type of account and how much you can contribute, see chapter 6.)

When you open your own IRA, set up automatic monthly contributions from your checking account so you can pay yourself first. Learning to pay yourself first is an integral part of becoming financially free.

9. MAKE YOUR MORTGAGE PAYMENT BIWEEKLY

If you pay your mortgage biweekly instead of monthly, you can knock off years of interest. Paying biweekly means you pay half of the stated mortgage every two weeks. For example, instead of paying $1,000 a month, you would pay $500 every two weeks.

Since there are twenty-six biweekly periods, paying biweekly means you make one extra payment a year, which results in a significant decrease in the time to payoff: a thirty-year loan converted to biweekly payments will be paid off in 310 months, or twenty-five years, ten months. You can reduce your loan period by nearly five years without changing anything besides when you make your payment. (Check with your lender to get the details.)

10. START A HEALTH PLAN

Starting a personal health and wellness plan changed my life. In 2018, I started walking every morning, and now I'm up to five miles a day. This is my therapy, my time to reflect on where I am and where I'm headed.

We have only one opportunity to do this thing called life and only one body to do it in. Take care of your body so you'll look good and feel good while you're enjoying financial freedom.

WHAT MONEY CAN DO

Money is only good for the good it can do. Money has allowed me to help others. I've had the great privilege of housing and feeding the homeless. I've been able to feed schoolchildren during the summer when they don't have meals at school. I've been able to help animal rescue groups care for animals and fight for animal rights. I've been able to support family members and friends in their time of need.

It feels so good to be able to help people or organizations— far better than going out and buying a Louis Vuitton handbag or a Rolex watch. It's like John Maxwell so eloquently said, "Success is great, but significance is where it's at." That's what financial freedom has done for me. It's given me significance and the opportunity to make a difference in people's lives.

What will financial freedom do for you?

Money will not give you contentment, joy, or peace. It will give you options to decide where you're going to live, how you're going to live, and what kind of things you can buy. Joy and peace come from within.

My hope is that you find your peace. Find how much money it will take to create the life that you've always dreamed of, and start building passive income streams so you can get there. As you move toward that goal, don't forget to enjoy the life you're living today because tomorrow isn't promised.

Financial freedom is a journey, not a destination. Enjoy the journey. It evolves and changes all along the way. Remember, the best things in life are not things; they are family and friends and time spent making memories together.

Good luck on your Financial Freedom journey. It's not easy, but it is simple and it is so worth it.

Acknowledgments

There are not enough words to express my gratitude toward the wonderful people who have made an impact on my life. Thank you from the bottom of my heart for always believing in me even when I didn't believe in myself.

First and foremost, to my amazing husband, Rick. You are the most patient and content person I know. These are two characteristics I have always wanted and searched for, so I am lucky to have found a soulmate who models them for me daily.

To my beautiful, loving mom. Thank you for encouraging me to believe that I could be whatever I wanted to be and for teaching me to enjoy the journey.

To my brother and sister. Thank you for making me tough growing up and for showing me the ropes. I love and appreciate you two a lot more now that I am all grown up.

To Brenda Benson, one of the most servant heart leaders I know. Thank you for your loyal, thought-provoking, collaborative, tear-jerking way of coaching me to be the best I can be. More importantly, thank you for your friendship!

To my Kentucky hometown girlfriends (you know who you are!). This is what true friendship is all about. Love you guys!

Jim and Linda McKissack, I'm so grateful for the opportunity you gave me to lead others. Thank you.

Thank you, Grant Sabatier, for your support, care, and candor.

To Chris, Randy, Heather, Jamie, Nick, and Milt. Thank you for allowing me to tell your stories in this book. You have been a great inspiration to those around you.

To my leadership teams in my offices. You are amazing inspirational leaders who bring your A game every day. I love being in business with you guys!

To all my readers and social media followers. Thank you for helping me get my message out. Thank you for allowing me to live in my passion.

Last but not least, thanks to the Scribe team for guiding me through my very first book. It has been an emotional journey. Thank you, Libby Allen, for guiding me every step of the way, and Erin Tyler, for my fabulous book cover. To my scribe, Gail Fay, you have made this so much easier than I thought or expected. I'm so grateful for your help and support all along the way.

Williams family, Thanksgiving 2019.

I am so grateful for my amazing family, who have
supported me and made me who I am today.

About the Author

MYRA OLIVER is a Kentucky girl who started her career as a hairstylist and became a real estate broker/investor and entrepreneur. She currently owns multiple Keller Williams Realty franchises.

After earning enough passive income through smart saving and real estate investments, Myra sold her hair salon and retired in her thirties. Three years later, she found her passion in helping others build their own streams of passive income through real estate investments.

Myra lives in Denton, Texas, with her husband, Rick, and their chihuahua, Izzy. To learn more about financial freedom and living your best life, visit her website, downhomemoney. com.

Notes

1   CareerBuilder, "Living Paycheck to Paycheck Is a Way of Life for Majority of U.S. Workers, according to New CareerBuilder Survey" (press release), CareerBuilder.com, August 24, 2017, https://press.careerbuilder. com/2017-08-24-Living-Paycheck-to-Paycheck-is-a-Way-of-Life-for-Majority-of-U-S-Workers-According-to-New-CareerBuilder-Survey.

2   "What Does It Mean When a Hawk Crosses Your Path," Dreaming and Sleeping, https://dreamingandsleeping.com/what-does-it-mean-when-a-hawk-crosses-your-path/.

3   "Here's How Seeing Hawks Often May Give Insight into Your Life," Power of Positivity, https://www.powerofpositivity.com/see-hawks-often-meaning-spirit-animal/.

4   Stephen C. Goss, "The Future Financial Status of the Social Security Program," *Social Security Bulletin* 70, no. 3 (2010): 111, ssa.gov/policy/docs/ssb/v70n3/ssb-v70n3.pdf.

5   Farmers' Almanac, "A Look Back at What Things Used to Cost," *Farmers' Almanac*, https://www.farmersalmanac.com/a-look-back-at-what-things-used-to-cost-18228.

6   Paul Davidson and Charisse Jones, "More Americans Go without Health Insurance for the First Time in a Decade," *USA Today*, September 10, 2019, https://www.usatoday.com/story/money/2019/09/10/median-household-income-stagnant-last-year-poverty-fell/2271025001/.

7   "U.S. Inflation Rate, $50,000 from 2017–2018," CPI Inflation Calculator, https://www.in2013dollars.com/2017-dollars-in-2018?amount=50000&future_pct=0.025.

8   "U.S. Life Expectancy 1950–2020," Macrotrends.net, https://www.macrotrends.net/countries/USA/united-states/life-expectancy.

9   Doreen McCallister, "Roger Bannister, First Runner to Break 4-Minute Mile Mark, Dies at 88," NPR, March 5, 2018, https://www.npr.org/sections/thetwo-way/2018/03/05/590792079/roger-bannister-first-runner-to-break-4-minute-mile-dies-at-88; Bill Taylor, "What Breaking the 4-Minute Mile Taught Us about the Limits of Conventional Thinking," *Harvard Business Review*, March 9, 2018, https://hbr.org/2018/03/what-breaking-the-4-minute-mile-taught-us-about-the-limits-of-conventional-thinking.

10 John Maxwell, *The 21 Irrefutable Laws of Leadership* (Nashville: Thomas Nelson, 1998), 1–10.

11 James Clear, "How Long Does It Actually Take to Form a New Habit? (Backed by Science)," JamesClear.com, https://jamesclear.com/new-habit.

12 Grant Sabatier, *Financial Freedom: A Proven Path to All the Money You Will Ever Need* (New York: Penguin Random House, 2019), 35.

13 Graph data taken from Kathleen Elkins, "These Four Charts Will Totally Change How You Think about Saving Money," CNBC: Make IT, September 27, 2017, https://www.cnbc.com/2017/09/27/nerdwallet-charts-show-the-power-of-compound-interest.html.

14 J. B. Maverick, "What Is the Average Annual Return for the S&P 500?" Investopedia, updated February 19, 2020, https://www.investopedia.com/ask/answers/042415/what-average-annual-return-sp-500.asp.

15 RBC Capital Markets, *Choosing a Sustainable Withdrawal Rate*, 2015, http://static.fmgsuite.com/media/documents/8c001261-5982-4312-8be9-f062f8d55924.pdf.

16 "Sixteen Tons" lyrics, Warner Chappell Music Inc. Royalty Network.

Made in the USA
Monee, IL
27 October 2020